CRY THE GOSPEL WITH YOUR LIFE

Religious Life in the Footsteps
of Brother Charles of Jesus

By

The Little Brothers and Little Sisters of Jesus

DIMENSION BOOKS INC.
DENVILLE NEW JERSEY 07834

Published by Dimension Books, Inc.
Denville, New Jersey 07834

ISBN 0-87193-152-4

TABLE OF CONTENTS

PART I

A SHORT BIOGRAPHY

ONE

A CHILD HEADED WRONG?
1858-1881

Charles de Foucauld did not have a peaceful, happy childhood. Born at Strasbourg on September 15, 1858, he was only five when his father, stricken with tuberculosis, left his family to go and live with his sister Inès in Paris. His mother took shelter with her father, Colonel de Morlet, bringing along her two children, Charles and Marie. Shortly afterward on March 3, 1864, she died of a miscarriage. Five months later, Monsieur de Foucauld died too, far from his children.

The grandfather then took charge of the two orphans. He was a believing Christian, upright and cultivated, but he was more than soft-hearted when it came to Charles, who brought back to him all the memories of his daughter. At the age of ten, the year he started classes at the Lycée of Strasbourg, Charles was an introverted boy who preferred to keep to himself. The death of his parents had made a deep imprint on his young, emotional personality and left him closed, aggressive, impatient, and hypersensitive.

His happiest times were vacations at the house of his aunt Inès. It was there that he got to know his cousin Marie, nine years his elder, a simple girl of deep goodness and faith. A great friendship grew up between them. Marie understood him and this helped him all through his years of wandering, as well as afterward in his religious life.

But the vacations did not last. 1870: the Franco-Prussian War, flight before the advancing enemy, unconditional surrender at Sedan, the siege of Paris, famine, civil war — all these events left deep traces in the sensitive twelve year old boy.

Two years later he would make his first communion. He had been well prepared and received it with earnest devotion. And yet, a few months later when school started in October, his second year at the lycee of Nancy, he entered on a deep religious crisis that was to last twelve years. Craving for knowledge, the solitary boy read everything he could find. His faith tottered, and he didn't come across a Christian who could give reasons for what he believed or answer his questions and doubts.

In his family only his cousin Marie could have been such a "mentor," but she married the year Charles was fifteen, and that strong tie that had bound him to her seemed in Charles's eyes to be broken.

Little by little Charles drifted away from the faith and from a Christian life. First he stopped going to church; later he in fact lost his faith. He didn't become an atheist but God was for him merely the Unknowable. It was only then that an uncaring moral slide began. Taciturn as ever, he became a decadent, lazy, self-indulgent youth.

At seventeen he decided to make a career of the army and followed the classical route: military academies Sainte-Genevieve and Saint-Cyr, then

cavalry school at Saumur, from which he graduated
in 1879, last in his class. His grandfather had died the
year before, and the last bond of affection that had
still held him back from wallowing in his dissipation
was broken. He got an appointment at Pont-à-
Mousson close to Nancy. He kept up the life of
pleasure he had been leading at Saumur but on a
grander scale, brashly running through his fortune. It
was not long before the whole town, with its pious
and soldierly traditions, was talking about the
extravagances of Lieutenant de Foucauld and his
scandals. He went from party to party, and yet he
would later say that in this period of his life he
experienced "a painful emptiness, a sadness such as I
have never felt."

At the end of 1880, his regiment was assigned to
Algeria. On the ship he brought along a casual lady-
friend, passing her off as the Viscountess de Foucauld. Once ashore, far from breaking off the pre-
tense, he broadcast his fling. Notified by his commanding officers to get rid of her, he balked, not out
of love for the lady, but out of pride. He didn't want
anyone meddling in his personal business. He had to
quit the army, and left with her for Evian, a resort
town near Switzerland. The social whirl was in full
swing. He did his best to drown himself in it, but more
unhappy than ever, he felt a deep disgust come over
him. He said, "I am a man for whom it's all over . . . "

TWO

A SEEKER
1881-1886

Three months later he learned that his former regiment was called to battle duty. With an astonishing capacity for rupture — this was a trait of his personality — he immediately left Evian and the easy life behind. He requested and obtained reinstatement in the army so that he could fight with his comrades.

The campaign in the Sahara south of Oran lasted eight months. During that time Charles conducted himself like a veteran soldier and a daring leader. He was a new man who surprised everyone. "He cheerfully puts up with the worst ordeals, spending himself constantly, looking out for his men with dedication," wrote the future General Laperrine, who was also there. The two men became friends on that expedition and remained so till the end.

His dip into the Sahara had unforeseen consequences. The contact with the Moslems made a deep impression on him. The battle over, he started studying Arabic. A new ambition surged up in him; to know these men and their lands at close range. He asked for a leave from the army to make an information-gathering excursion. Denied. He turned in his resignation and left the army.

The idea came to him to explore Morocco, great land to the west, unknown and mysterious. He prepared himself for the trip for a year and a half, diligently studying applied astronomy, topography, Arabic, and everything that had been written on Morocco. Nothing was too much for him. This twenty-three year old whom everyone had considered lazy and debauched had a compelling need to rise in his own estimation and to redeem himself in the eyes of others, particularly his family.

At last he left Algiers on June 30, 1883, resolved to go to the end no matter what, and explore this closed country where no European had really yet penetrated. When he came back after eleven months of danger and adventure, risking death more than once, he remarked to a friend, "It was tough but very interesting, and I succeeded." Those few words are enough to sum up all his tenacity and strength of will to get what he was after.

He came back from Morocco a transformed man. During his travels he had led a rugged existence and endured humiliations, mockery and insult (for it was disguised as a Palestinian Jew that he had penetrated Morocco, where Jews were tolerated as a despised minority). He had also discovered the brotherly hospitality of the Jews he met and had taken part in their prayers. He had been struck by the faith of the Moslems and the simple prayer of these men for whom "God is Great."

He would ponder these discoveries a long time, but without harvesting the fruits of them right away. He, the unbeliever, seeking after human discoveries, had met men for whom God counted more than all else.

His life became serious and austere as he worked

on the preparation of his travel journal, *Reconnaissance in Morocco*. A solitary life with "a taste for classical pagan virtues," he would later say of it. He divided his time between Paris and Algiers, making an excursion in the Algerian desert as far south as El-Goléa and then coming back through Tunisia to increase his knowledge. He seriously thought of marriage to a young lady of Algiers, but his family called him back to France.

The friendship that bound him to his cousin Marie, who had become Madame de Bondy, obliged him to ask himself basic questions. Here was a woman whose intelligence he admired, and the depth of her faith was clear to him. She introduced him to her family friend, Father Huvelin, a sure guide and a man of prayer and deep learning.

An inner force was driving Charles. Though he didn't believe in anything, he started going to churches, feeling restless anywhere but there. He would spend long hours there repeating his odd prayer, "My God, if You exist, make me know You."

THREE

GOD ALONE
1886-1901

One October morning in 1886, Brother Charles set out to find Father Huvelin. He would ask him for some "scientific information" about religion. As he had studied Arabic and geography, he would study Christianity, continuing his explorations. Father Huvelin was in his parish church, St. Augustine's, hearing confessions as he spent many hours doing each day. Charles entered the confessional without kneeling, merely leaning over to speak to the priest and say he had come to ask some questions. "What you need to do," said Father Huvelin, "is kneel down and make your confession."

Charles accepted and the light came. He received from Father Huvelin God's forgiveness of his sins and the Bread of Life. A total and unconditional conversion. "As soon as I believed there was a God, I realized that I could do nothing else but live solely for Him. My religious vocation dates from the same hour as my faith. God is so Great . . . "[1]

He was 28 years old.

Days, then months went by. He was deeply happy. His new-found faith flooded his life and joy exploded within him. Then began a long quest: how was he to give himself to God? He wanted to be a monk. Rather than tell him about the different Orders, Father Huvelin gave him the Gospel to read. And from then on what Charles wanted to do was to imitate Jesus. He sought avidly in the Gospels all the actions and gestures of the Lord to meditate on, steep himself in, and conform to. But how was he to translate concretely into his life this desire for imitation? He groped in the dark, tense, even sorrowful, ardently asking God for the light.

God would give it to him the year he was thirty, in 1888, leading him gradually by progressive steps.

He heard Father Huvelin say in a sermon, "Jesus so took the last place that no one has ever gotten it away from Him." After that, he represented Jesus to himself as the One who, out of love, made Himself the servant of all. That was where Charles wanted to be with Him, he who up until then had looked for the first place.

On a visit with his cousin Marie to the Trappist monastery of Fontgombault, he happened to cross the path of a lay brother in a very worn out habit. It was a revelation for Charles. This unknown brother became a concrete model for his search for the last place.

Father Huvelin asked him to make a pilgrimage to the Holy Land. Without enthusiasm he obeyed and set out as a solitary pilgrim. He came back carried away, having discovered the real-life features of Jesus in the land where He had lived.

From then on he knew how he would imitate Christ: in the poverty of a very simple life, the life of Nazareth.

After making several retreats, he chose the Trappists and said goodbye to his family. The bonds of friendship between him and Mme. de Bondy had been growing all this time, and to say goodbye forever truly tore him apart. "A sacrifice that cost me all my tears," he would later call it, "The wound of January 15 is the same as ever." He arrived at the monastery of Our Lady of the Snows in south central France (not far from Viviers) on January 16, 1890. There he was given the name Brother Marie Albéric. He knew that in six months he would go on to a daughter foundation, the abbey of Our Lady of the Sacred Heart in Akbès, Syria, where he had asked to be sent because he thought to find the greatest possible poverty there. It was hardly more than a barn, made of rough planks and branches and covered with a thatched roof.

For seven years he put all his heart into being a monk, faithful to his work and his prayer. Yet something didn't suit him. He wrote, "We are poor in the eyes of the rich, but we aren't poor the way our Lord was, poor the way I was in Morocco, poor the way St. Francis was." One day a workman from the village died and Brother Marie Albéric was sent to pray by his coffin. "What a difference between his house and where we live. I long for Nazareth." He began writing a rule with the idea of founding a religious community that he wanted to call the Little Brothers of Jesus. But Father Huvelin answered him that his rule was terrifying and unlivable. He allowed Charles to follow his desires but told him not to write a rule for others.

His superiors sent him for a few weeks to the monastery of Staweli in Algeria and then to Rome to do his religious studies. But in fact they kept him there only a few months and they agreed that he leave the Order to live the way he wanted to — in poor workers' conditions, "the life of Nazareth." Had he made a mistake in entering the monastery? In a sense, yes, for it didn't bring him what he was looking for and he had to leave it to be true to his vocation. But he had needed a monastic formation, which the Trappists gave him, and he was never to think that his years in the monastery were a useless detour.

He set out for the Holy Land. It was in the town of Nazareth itself that he was to inaugurate his new life. For three years he was a handy man at the convent of Poor Clare Nuns there, spending long hours praying when his work was done, kneeling before the tabernacle of their chapel, reading the Bible and writing out his meditations. He did everything he could not to be known by his origins of class and nation and went by the name of Brother Charles of Jesus.

The nuns wanted him to become a priest. He rejected the idea at first, thinking it would take him away from his position of humility and littleness. Then he realized that priesthood was not necessarily incompatible with poverty. Being a priest would allow him to live out his love of the Eucharist more fully. It would be useful if he was to found a congregation. In the end he accepted the idea and returned to France.

He went back to Our Lady of the Snows, the Trappist monastery where he had started out ten years earlier, to prepare for the priesthood. During his retreats before his ordination as a deacon and then as a priest, he saw clearly the path to follow. He gave up the idea of going back to settle in the Holy Land, though he loved it exceedingly there, as well as the idea of being a hermit. He would go where the most forsaken people were, to the Sahara or to Morocco, the lands he had known in his youth, those vast expanses without a single priest.

On June 9, 1901, he was ordained at Viviers, France. Two extremes had long since taken possession of him, absolute love of God and total dedication to the people who were farthest from God. From then on these two poles would meet in a single love, which would send him out, spur him onward, and finally bring him to give the greatest proof of love possible, to lay down his life for his friends.

He rummaged through his past as an unbeliever to find the place where he should live out his priesthood. The nomads he had known in Morocco represented for him "the farthest away" from the Gospel. Waiting for the frontiers of Morocco to open up, he sought the best situated point on the southern border, "somewhere between Ain Sefra and Touat," he said, "some garrison without a priest, so that I can live there as a silent cloistered monk, praying and administering the sacraments."

Having gotten permission from his bishop to go and live in Africa, he left France immediately without even taking time to see anyone but his sister.

FOUR

AT THE HEART OF THE WORLD
1901-1916

When he got off the boat at Algiers on September 10, 1901, he was 45 years old. He was at the "noontime" of his religious life. It was 15 years since his conversion. He had 15 years still to live, the years in which he would be fully himself. An old comrade from cavalry school was working at the Governor General's Office in Algiers, so from him he could obtain the necessary authorizations to go south and live in the Sahara. France was then in the process of colonizing Algeria, and the Saharan regions were not open to civilian settlers yet.

Beni-Abbès

When he got to Beni-Abbès on October 28, 1901, he chose at a short distance from the oasis a little hollow by the wadi, barren but irrigable. Soldiers from the garrison helped him build his hermitage: a chapel, three cells and a guest room. Down the slope of the hill he made a garden among a few palm trees growing wild there.

He called his hermitage "the fraternity" and got people to call him Brother Charles. He wanted to be a man of prayer and a man of brotherhood. He spent hours of the day and of the night in his chapel kneeling before the tabernacle. He wanted to befriend everyone so that all would consider him their brother: Moslems or Christians, enlisted men or officers, Arabs or blacks, slaves or freemen, travellers or villagers. Very quickly the hermitage filled up with people who came to see him and speak to him. He noted, "The fraternity is very quiet at night and from 10 a.m. to 3 p.m. But it's a beehive from 5 to 8 a.m. and 4 to 8 p.m."[1]

Brother Charles ran into a brutal reality: slavery. Officially it had been abolished in Algeria, but in the south, in an effort to appease the local chieftains and not stir up trouble certain French authorities had let the emancipation of the slaves go for awhile. Brother Charles spoke out vigorously against that cowardice disguised as prudence, that hypocrisy that kept in place a long-standing shame. To make it worse, the condition of the slaves in the region was wretched; they were starved, beaten, abused, and if they tried to escape, mutilated.

He raised his cry of indignation in season and out of season, addressing himself to officers, to his bishop, and to his friends in France. He wanted the subject brought before public opinion by means of a debate in Parliament. He got no immediate result and for the time being his cry seemed stifled. And so, he ransomed slaves one by one and set them free, whenever his family or friends sent him some money.

Had Brother Charles at last found in his hermitage at Beni-Abbès the definitive form of his dedication? No. Events would come and shake up the monastic structure he had given to his life, pushing him outside his cloister wall.

In fact Brother Charles had come to Beni-Abbes hoping to move on into Morocco. The French Army was gradually getting ready to advance westward, but it was not on their power that Brother Charles wanted to go. He was hoping that some of the Moroccan traders he made friends with at Beni-Abbès would be able to take him back to their country with their caravans.

But the borders remained closed. And so when his friend Laperrine, commanding officer of the Region of the Oases, began to speak to him about the Tuaregs, far to the south, Brother Charles heard in it the Lord calling him to another people "to whom no one else can go if I do not." There were several Tuareg tribes in the rocky plateaus of the Hoggar; they were hereditary enemies to the Arabs, fiercely independent nomads, who had had hardly any contact with Europeans. Two of Brother Charles's personal friends had died in consequence of Tuareg attacks. In June 1903, Laperrine wrote telling him of meeting a Tuareg woman of renowned kindness who had saved the lives of several wounded Arab soldiers in 1881, when a mission led by Colonel Flatters to explore a route for the Trans-Saharan Railway was tricked and massacred. This letter stirred Brother Charles's desire still more.

He decided to join the first convoy, set for September 6. But there was fighting close to Beni-Abbès, and he chose to stay inside where he might be needed. Brother Charles was always looking for the Will of God in the cue of events. It had overturned his cloistered life-style, and now it overturned his plans too.

Toward the Hoggar

In December another letter from Laperrine made him change his mind again. A convoy was leaving for the south on January 10, 1904. He grabbed the chance, for in this "land of hunger and thirst" people didn't travel alone but in caravan with camels and donkeys to carry water, food and baggage. The long days' marches took them week after week, from one rare watering place to another in the scanty scrub lands, avoiding as much as possible the zones where there was no life at all.

At Adrar he met up with Laperrine, who told him that three of the six big Tuareg tribes had accepted French rule the year before, among them the Hoggars, the most important tribe. Laperrine promised to take him along the following month as he went through their territory. In the meantime Brother Charles went to Akabli, an ideal place to learn Tamashaq, the Tuareg language. There were people living there who spoke it and numerous Tuareg caravans passing through.

Laperrine let him join a 500 mile tour through the newly subjugated regions, stopping here and there in Tuareg camps or grazing grounds. It was a peaceful expedition and Brother Charles was happy. He discovered the Tuaregs and took to them from the bottom of his heart. "The Tuaregs are turning out to be very sociable and open," he wrote, and he did his best to win their friendship, simply and openly.

The trip ended at In-Salah, and at the end of January 1905 one year later, he finally got back to Beni-Abbès.

Right away he took up his monastic life again, thinking to live that way a long time, with hours of prayer in the Eucharistic presence, reports on his trip among the Tuaregs, numerous visits from local people and passing soldiers. He had no time to work in his garden in spite of his desires.

In April Laperrine invited him with insistence to spend the summer in the Hoggar. With the permission of his bishop, he left at the beginning of May. In June he met Moussa ag Amastane, chieftain of the Hoggar Tuaregs, who had come out with the leading notables of his people to meet the French detachment. The two caravans stayed together a fortnight. Brother Charles could thus get acquainted with Moussa and ask him for hospitality. Together they examined the different possibilities for where he would live and agreed on Tamanrasset, which he reached on August 11, 1905.

What was his ideal now for his life? That of Jesus at Nazareth in everything and for everything. "No habit, no cloister, no withdrawn dwellings, no large expenses . . . but extreme poverty in everything, like Jesus at Nazareth. The life of Nazareth can be led anywhere. Lead it where it is most useful for your fellow men."

The Last Eleven Years at Tamanrasset

The soldiers had left Tamanrasset and he was alone in the midst of the Tuaregs. The closest Frenchmen were 400 miles away at In-Salah. Peace had just been established in the region.

The village was located right at the heart of the Hoggar at an altitude of 5000 feet. It was nothing but twenty huts scattered over two miles. On the other hand there were many nomads in the surrounding area, for the tribe's strongest center was here. He began to build his fraternity, but he no longer had the same plans and ideas as at Beni-Abbès. He would build merely a simple stone and earth house, 20 feet long and 5 feet wide, inside which was his chapel, his bedroom-workroom with a wattle shelf that served him as bed and table, and the entrance way used for storage. Outside, a hut and a covered place for cooking. Later on he would have a second hut built, and in 1910 he added a few feet to the length of the house.

He knew that in these regions someone living alone became more approachable, but in fact people didn't come to see him often at the beginning. So he put all his energy into the study of Tamashaq. At first he thought it would take him only a few months' work, but the unremitting labor of his whole lifetime was not to be enough to finish the undertaking. For three months he had the help of a friend, Motylinski, a professor of Arabic and Berber who agreed to come all the way to Tamanrasset. They went north together on September 12, 1906.

Reaching Beni-Abbès, he stayed there only a few days while he made his yearly retreat. He set out for Algiers, by way of Ain Sefra. At Algiers in the house of the White Fathers, he met his first companion, Brother Michel, and set out with him jubilantly toward Beni-Abbès and the Hoggar. On the trip he wrote this prayer, "If it is Your Will, establish this year the Little Brothers of the Sacred Heart of Jesus . . . " He stopped at In-Salah in February 1907. It was then that he realized his first companion was not cut out for it, and he sent him back to Algiers. More bad news reached him: Motylinski had died. He would have to go on alone with the work they had started. It was this that kept him on at In-Salah, where he compiled his first dictionary. Afterwards he made a rapid trip to Tamanrasset and continued on southward with a scientific mission going that way. It gave him the opportunity to visit the country and meet a great many nomads.

July 1907 he was back at Tamanrasset, in solitude once more. Until then, thanks to the Frenchmen he was with as he travelled, he had always had someone to serve his Masses, for he had no authorization to celebrate Mass alone. Now he could expect only rare visits from Christians. He knew it and lucidly chose to remain in the Hoggar deprived of mass — a sacrifice for him — rather than not stay on there.

When he got there he found them in the grips of a terrible drought. It had not rained for seventeen months. The goats, chief resource of the country, were as dry as the ground. People were hungry. Despite his increasing exhaustion, Brother Charles took on several specific projects for the future of the Hoggar, working hand in hand with Moussa ag Amastane, the Amenokal of the Tuaregs he had become friends with. But what took him more time were his linguistic undertakings, which he worked on from sunrise to sunset with Ba-Hamou, his Tamashaq informant, whom he paid a high price and whose time and patience were limited.

Christmas 1907. No Mass. No mail in three months. No visitors either. In spite of these sufferings, convinced that prayer and self-sacrifice were his principal means of action, he peacefully accepted his life of solitude. A few days later he fell sick. Lack of food and sleep combined with overwork had brought him down. He had to interrupt his work for a month and change his plan of going to Beni-Abbes.

At the end of January, good news. He received from Rome authorization to celebrate Mass alone. It was a great day long awaited. But he was not authorized to reserve the Blessed Sacrament. Until 1914 his tabernacle remained empty. During his sickness he discovered the friendship and loyalty of his neighbors. His health returned and his life went back to normal. He had just passed through one of the most important moments of his life.

His second stay at Tamanrasset lasted until Christmas 1908. On that day he left (stopping over at In-Salah, El-Goléa and Ghardaia) for France, where he had not returned for seven years. He spent three weeks with his family, and saw his cousin Marie de Bondy for the first time in nineteen years. He laid the groundwork for an association of Christian lay people along the lines of the spirituality he would have put at the base of the religious congregations he dreamed of founding: to live as contemplatives in the midst of the world.

He got back to Tamanrasset on June 11, 1909, after a month's stay at Beni-Abbès. He went back to sedentary life, alone, with no companion on the horizon. Between times he made two tours with Laperrine around the camps and villages in a radius of more than 60 miles. These visits were a way for Brother Charles to get to know people he did not see at Tamanrasset and befriend them. He got the idea of making houses in other places besides at Tamanrasset so as to live closer to the nomads. Only one of his projects did he accomplish: a hermitage at Assekrem. He had lost his heart to this mountain, 8000 feet high, 40 miles north of Tamanrasset in the center of the Ahaggar range. He thought from them on to divide his time between these two fraternities in the Hoggar and the one in Beni-Abbès.

1910. This year left a great emptiness for him. He lost three great friendships. Bishop Guérin died at

the age of 37, worn out by Sahara life. "His passing
has left a great gap." On August 15 he learned of the
death of Father Huvelin, his guide for so many years.
"It is shattering for me," he wrote. In November his
friend Colonel Laperrine, after nine years in com-
mand, was assigned to France. He and Brother
Charles were never to see each other again in the
Sahara. These three losses left an imprint on him. For
though Brother Charles loved solitude and his austere
and rugged life, he was a man who needed others,
who needed friends. He lived to the full the paradox
that defines a man of the Sahara, who must count on
others to survive when he is alone. From the recesses
of his desert Brother Charles's life cries out to modern
man that to live we need both solitude with the
Beloved and friendship with our brothers.

1911. Except for a second brief trip to France at
the beginning of the year, aimed chiefly at making
known his association for lay people, Brother Charles
did not leave the Hoggar this year nor the following
one. In July he went up to the Assekrem with supplies
for sixteen months. In this relative solitude he could
spend more time studying Tamashaq with Ba-Hamou
his informant. On this arid peak he was like Noah in
his ark, setting out on a long voyage with no ports of
call. But he found himself headed home sooner than
planned, for Ba-Hamou was so miserable there that
Brother Charles promised to let him leave for
Christmas.

With his eyes on "the most beautiful scenery in
nature," he loved to feel himself alone with God in
this wild and awesome setting, a forest of rocky crags
and spikes, sterile mountains bathed in the light of a
marvelously limpid sky, creation's beauty and immensity, a mirror of the Beauty of God.

But he also had occasion to practice hospitality. Without seeing large numbers of people, he received visits from nomads who were camping two or three days' walk from Assekrem and would come to spend the day with him. Back in Tamanrasset on December 15, where he found things in a frightful state of destitution, his neighbors welcomed him gladly. For a time had gone on, his relations with the Tuaregs had become more and more solid and sincere. Friendships had grown, and so had his familiarity with the country, its customs and its people, unknown to him before. And naturally they took up more and more of his time. He also received visits from French officers passing through the region; with some of them he kept up a considerable correspondence. They asked advice and consulted him on a wide range of subjects.

What was Brother Charles's attitude toward the phenomenon he was immersed in, a colonial empire in full expansion? To understand his place, the question must first be asked, what sort of presence had he wanted to have at the heart of this world caught up in change?

Coming to the Sahara, he could not have had a hidden presence in the sense he had once dreamed of at the monastery or at Nazareth when he meditated on the thirty years of hidden life of the Lord. At that time and in that context, and considering who he had been, he could not help being in close contact with the officers of the Saharan army, his former comrades. It was the only way he could get permission to live in those regions. However, once settled, he could have cut himself off from this world and lived the life of a hermit entirely occupied with seeking God alone in prayer and silence, "dead to the world," shutting his eyes to everything around him.

In fact from the outset that was not what he chose. On the contrary he wanted to keep his door wide open — and his eyes wide open — to let the sufferings of men enter into his heart. In a word, he wanted to be a "universal brother." And that intention was to oblige him to take a position on the political questions of that age of rapid mutation when colonial conquest was overturning ancestral structures.

Theoretically, the individual problems of each one of his guests could have been separate from political problems. In fact they were not. French officers and Tuaregs alike spoke of all that concerned them with Brother Charles. Everything was connected and interwoven. It was because they were aware of his knowledge of the Tuaregs and his influence with them that officers came to ask him questions and talk over their plans and their difficulties. But it was true the other way around, too. Because they knew how much attention Laperrine and the others listened to him with, the Tuaregs came to tell him about their grievances, asking him to plead their case with their new masters, whether about things that had been requisitioned, or services they had not been paid for, or other violations against their possessions or their dignity.

Both sides appreciated his competence, his fairness and his justice, and so put a growing trust in him. He became a sort of moral arbiter, not officially but by general unspoken agreement. From our distance in another era and another place, his role may seem abnormal, but in his time and place that role was ratified by all concerned — Tuaregs, slaves and French officers — who were one and all his friends.

Thus it was that he who had left all to follow Christ at the lowest place became, without having sought it, the friend and counsellor of Moussa and of Laperrine. Not a notable nor an officer came to Tamanrasset who didn't pay him a visit. And he who had left the monastery so as not to have "a life of honored learning," and had gone to live at Nazareth as the humblest of manual workers, launched into a work of linguistics and ethnography. Already at Beni-Abbès intellectual work had taken a good deal of his time from manual work. In the Hoggar his hermitage was full of books, notes and manuscripts from which would come grammars, dictionaries, and anthologies of proverbs and poetry.

Had he deviated from the path of his vocation? No. For him obscurity and "lowliness," as he called it, were only a means. The end was brotherhood, a fellowship of sharing the life and the fate of his brothers, the people of the Sahara, simply because they were his brothers — and especially with the poorest among them toward whom he would always be particularly attentive. The change in his life style cannot be explained as secular life usurping from religious life. Rather it was light from his religious life flooding his social and scientific activities. The foundation stone of his life was always the same, a will to live the life of Nazareth. Enough to see his quarters at Beni-Abbès or in the Hoggar to understand that for him Nazareth was a down-to-earth experience. The influence that is his after his death does not give us the right to forget how far from easy his daily life was in the solitudes of the desert.

1913. After a trip to France with Ouksem, a 22 year-old Tuareg boy, he came back to the Hoggar for the beginning of winter. A prolonged drought had made the nomads lose four-fifths of their goats and half of their camels. That spurred them to plant gardens, build houses and in short become nearly sedentary. A promising step forward for them, Brother Charles was well aware, and he was glad of it as he was glad of whatever good happened in the line of human development for his people. He never separated human progress from openings to spiritual values.

While in Europe the storm was brewing and finally broke out in August 1914, life in the desert remained untroubled, and Brother Charles was able to write on July 21, 1914, "The Hoggar, so long the repair of bandits, has become a country of great peace and great calm."

1916. The war came closer with the Italian-Turkish combats in Ajjer, the Moroccan raiding parties grew more and more numerous in Adrar; and abruptly with the seizure of Djanet on March 24 by the Senoussis, the Hoggar was directly threatened. Brother Charles got places of refuge in the mountains ready for the civilians, with the army's cooperation. In addition he built at Tamanrasset a bordj, which is to say a little fort, to be a refuge in case of raid for his poor and undefended friends of the village. It was a square construction about 45 feet on a side, solidly built of dried earth with walls 3 feet thick. On June 2 he went to live in the bordj, which wasn't yet finished. He was asked to store there six cases of ammunition and thirty rifles. On September 20 everyone at Tamanrasset rushed to take refuge at the bordj, but it was a false alarm. On November 15 the construction was completed.

Friday, the first of December. It was the evening of a splendid winter day. Brother Charles was alone.

The mail would be arriving. He had written five letters that day, including one to his sister. To one of his friends he had just written, "We must never hesitate to ask for posts where the danger, the self-sacrifice and the dedication are the greatest . . . " To his cousin Marie, "When we are reduced to nothing, it is the most powerful means we have of being united to Jesus and doing good to souls . . . "

Forty men came up to the bordj in silence. There were Senoussis and Tuaregs. The Tuaregs had brought along a man who knew Brother Charles's habits. In the gathering night he called Brother Charles saying he had brought the mail. Brother Charles opened the door. He was immediately seized, thrown to the ground and tied with his hands behind his back. They interrogated him. He kept silence. A 15 year old boy was set to guard him. The others went inside, looting the hermitage, making away with the arms. Suddenly a cry, "The Arabs!" In fact, two camel-mounted soldiers were coming up. Shots. The boy panicked, turned his gun on his prisoner and fired. Brother Charles sank to the ground without a cry, killed instantly.

The two soldiers were also killed. The raiders spent the night in the bordj. As they were leaving the next morning, they saw a third camel rider approaching. They killed him. It was he who was bringing the mail.

FIVE

HIS MESSAGE

Brother Charles died alone. It was the grain of wheat that falls to the ground in silence so as to come to life afterward and bear much fruit.[1]

He had meditated on martyrdom since 1897 and desired it faithfully. One day he had written, "Whatever the reason for which we may be killed, if we receive an unjust and cruel death as a blessed gift from Your hand and a joyous occasion to imitate You, if we offer it to You as a whole-hearted sacrifice and do not resist in order to obey Your word, then we will die for pure love. If it is not a martyrdom in the strict sense of the word and in the eyes of men, it will be one in Your eyes and a very faithful image of Your death . . . "

In many ways Brother Charles's destiny was singular and altogether inimitable. He lived at a unique moment of history and occupied a place in it only he could have held. No priest in his time could have penetrated so deep into the Sahara without Brother Charles's background, or could have stayed there without his unique combination of gifts.

Some have regretted that he should have had to give his witness in the midst of a colonial conquest and be compromised with the military. There is no way out for any of us, no one is an island and we are all part and parcel of the history of mankind. The more someone is impelled to commit himself to the real life of men in the name of brotherhood, the more he must carry the weight of the contradictions of that life. Brother Charles lived on the paths of men, and when their path was tragic, he showed how far brotherhood can go, even when it is denied, in its humble and magnificent power.

Singular and inimitable too was the way Brother Charles lived poverty. On the one hand he had a vision of the life of Nazareth that called for living solely by the humble work of his hands, yet he himself was never to realize it and always received most of his support from his family in France. And on the other hand his physical endurance in fasting and exertion betray a special gift where others cannot ordinarily follow his example. But in his highly personal way, he went out ahead in the ideal of Gospel poverty he had glimpsed, and what is inimitable in his life has the ring of a prophet's cry.

Beyond his personal destiny, what new path does he open for us all? He had searched for it for fifteen years (before, during and after his time at the monastery) doggedly, arduously, even agonizingly.

Here is his own explanation: "'Whatever you do to one of the least of these, you do it to Me.'[2] I think there is no verse in the Gospel that has made a deeper impression on me and transformed my life more . . . " Transformed his life — from the day of his conversion, his whole life was a passionate protest against spiritual unrealism. "I cannot conceive of love without a need, a compelling need for conforming, for resembling, and above all for sharing all the sorrows and hardships of the life of the one I love." His example was Jesus of Nazareth who made his own the poverty of the poor of His village.

"Whatever you do to one of the least of these." Seeking God, he found Him really only when he was among the most dispossessed, in fact partaking in their life to the point of becoming one of their own, until finally he died alone one evening, in the name of all his people. It was the love of Christ that impelled him to a life of fellowship for the sake of building brotherhood. But there is another fellowship, that of the Body of Christ, which consecrates the brotherhood of men as they come to know themselves sons of God and brothers of Christ. That was why he wanted the Eucharist at the heart of his life as it was at the heart of his hermitage. For him there was an indissoluble bond between these two great pronouncements of Jesus: "This is My Body given for you,"[3] and "Whatever you do to the least of My brothers, you do it to Me."

Presence to Christ in the Eucharist and presence to Christ in the poor: these are the two pillars, interlocking and unshakable, on which Brother Charles's life rested. He gave up leading this life of his in the Holy Land, for he felt himself driven to "live Nazareth where it is most useful for my fellowmen." Taking the route of the desert, the route of naked faith and pure hope, he consecrated himself to an extreme task and set out alone on a long and difficult road, knowing he would not see the end of it: the road of preparing hearts to know and love God better.

A new path was opening up in the Church for living the Gospel counsels in close fellowship with the life of the poor.

PART II

BROTHER CHARLES' SPIRITUALITY
FOR RELIGIOUS LIFE

"Do all I can to found and spread the
Little Brothers and the Little Sisters
of the Sacred Heart of Jesus."

This was one of Brother Charles's resolutions.
With these words or others like them he made this
resolution at retreat after retreat. It shows he had
made founding these congregations one of the goals
of his life. And yet at his death in 1916, he was alone.
He had not founded a single community. He cannot,
then, be called a founder in the strict sense the word
usually has in the Church. Nonetheless there exist
today several religious congregations of men and
women that hark back to him and consider him the
father of the spirituality and the style of religious life
they have adopted. Each congregation has a direct
founder who has had a personal role in giving it a
specific orientation. Each has a history, however
short, and is marked with a distinct personality
through its own experience. But beyond these things,
the congregations have a family likeness and share a
certain spirit, called the spirit of the Fraternity. It is a
spirit, besides, which is broader than these religious
congregations and overflows in one way or another to
secular institutes and other groups and to all who
have ties with Brother Charles.

The pages that follow will attempt to say something about that spirit. More precisely, they will
evoke some of the events of Charles de Foucauld's life
and quote his writings at length in order to get at the
chief values that men and women have recognized
and admired in him. These values mold the religious
life that is theirs and give them a guiding light for
understanding and living out the Gospel vocation
they hear themselves called to today. The question

is simply this: what is religious life for little brothers or little sisters? Put it another way: what is the connection between the "Fraternities" and Brother Charles?

Though we are writing about the meaning of Brother Charles's story for religious life, we have not intended to deny the lay groups who find their inspiration in Him and rightly read his story differently at certain points. We offer merely a sharing of our experience as little brothers and little sisters, and tell what Brother Charles has given us for a way of religious life in his footsteps.

ONE

TO LIVE ONLY FOR GOD

On August 14, 1901, Charles de Foucauld wrote to his friend Henry de Castries:[1]

As soon as I believed there was a God, I knew I could not do anything else but live only for Him. My vocation to religious life dates from the same hour as my faith. How great God is! There is such a difference between God and everything that is not Him!

In its beginnings my faith had a good many obstacles to conquer. I had doubted so much that I didn't believe everything in a day. First it was the miracles in the Gospel that I considered unbelievable. Then it was that I wanted to mix in passages of the Koran with my prayers. But God's grace and my confessor's advice cleared away the fog.

I wanted to be a religious and to live for God alone. I wanted to do the most perfect thing whatever it might be. My confessor made me wait three years. As for myself, though I longed to "breathe out my life before God in sheer losing of myself," as Bossuet says, I did not know what Order to choose. The Gospel showed me that "the first commandment is to love God with all your heart,"[2] and that everything had to be enfolded in love. Everyone knows that love's first effect is imitation. Therefore I was to enter the Order where I would find the most exact imitation of JESUS. I didn't feel I was made to imitate His public life of preaching; thus I ought to imitate His hidden life as a poor and humble workman at Nazareth. It seemed to me that no one offered me this life better than the Trappists.

I loved very fondly what family the Lord had left me. I wanted to make a sacrifice, to be like Him who made so many, and I left home — it's been nearly twelve years ago now — for a Trappist monastery in Armenia. I spent six and a half years there. Then, desiring a deeper dispossession and a greater lowliness so that I might be still more like Jesus, I went to Rome and received permission from the Superior General of the Order to go to Nazareth and live there without anyone knowing who I was, as a workman living by my daily labor. I stayed there four years, withdrawn from the world in a blessed solitude and inward prayerfulness, tasting the joys of that poverty and lowliness God had made me desire so ardently in order that I might imitate Him. Exactly a year ago I took the road back for France on my confessor's advice in order to receive Holy Orders. I was just ordained a priest and I'm applying now to go to the Sahara where I would continue "the hidden life of Jesus at Nazareth." I don't mean to preach but to live in the solitude, the poverty and the humble labor of Jesus, while trying to do good to souls not with my words but with prayer, the offering of the Holy Sacrifice, penance and the practice of charity.

It was fifteen years after his conversion when Brother Charles wrote these lines, and he had just been ordained a priest. He had already come a certain way since recovering his faith, but he knew and asserted that it was from the very first instant when this faith burst once more into his heart that he had been totally taken hold of by an imperative sense of God, the Absolute of Love. That is what he means when he says, "live only for Him," or, "breathe out my life before God in sheer losing of myself."

God alone. This imperative is at the heart of every consecrated life. No matter what may be the signs, the pathways or the detours that God uses to guide a destiny, no matter what the service He calls for or what tasks He leads someone to, no one can speak of a religious vocation if there is not some intuition of this Absolute. A person's heart must have begun to vibrate with the first tones of that "live only for God."

Moreover, those who sense such a call cannot but discover in time, and in the very measure in which they recognize what it is, that this "God alone" consecrates them to the love of their brothers and sisters. How could it be otherwise, when this call sets them in the footsteps of Jesus?

A vocation can reveal itself in an instant of light that sweeps up the decision in its flood. Or it can be discovered slowly through a long experience of service to others, or else as a secret reality which has lain buried in someone's heart for as long as he or she has existed. As intense as the first light may be, even if as in the case of Brother Charles it sets the whole direction of a life in an instant, that light never dispenses someone from the long learning process in which he finds out what "to live only for God" means in his everyday life. Speaking of his stay in the Trappist monastery, Brother Charles tells us he went through this apprenticeship:

> To be alone with God in the universe is the first lesson Father Polycarp taught me, and I bless him for that lesson. Thanks to it I pass by without seeing, or at least without stopping.[3]

However generous may be the first élan this call draws forth — for such a light is itself a call — giving a total response will always be the affair of a whole lifetime, and it will also be quite an everyday affair. Each day will have to reach toward a response to the invitation, lived in faithfulness and self-surrender. "As soon as I believed there was a God, I knew I could not do anything else but live only for Him alone," Brother Charles told us. If his words touch us, it is because they evoke something pure and absolute. It is also because the life of the one who wrote them, given day after day, does not belie them. They have the strength of proven authenticity. Things that ring true touch hearts. Reading Brother Charles's life, the jolt of discovering his personal response to God's call has been for a good number of little brothers and little sisters, especially among the first to join, one of the means the Lord took to make them, too, hear His call and guide them to discover their own vocation. That is one of the first things we owe Brother Charles.

Drawn from Brother Charles's meditations, this prayer will be suggestive for those whose way of responding to God may be like his. This is what Brother Charles wanted to make of his life and aimed at each day with the deepest desires of his heart and with his actions as well:

Father,
I abandon myself into Your hands,
do with me what You will.
For whatever You may do, I thank You.
I am ready for all, I accept all,
let only Your will be done in me,
as in all Your creatures:
I wish no more than this, O Lord.
Into Your hands I commend my soul.
I offer it to You with all the love of my heart.
For I love, You, my God,
and so need to give myself,
to surrender myself into Your hands without reserve
and with boundless confidence,
for You are my Father.

TWO

TO IMITATE JESUS OUT OF LOVE

On January 15, 1890, a little more than three years after his conversion, Charles de Foucauld left his family. The next day he entered the Trappist monastery of Our Lady of the Snows. The separation was a painful one, more so than might have been expected for a man of his stamp, but this leave-taking was the consequence of the choice he had already made at the hour of his conversion and which had been ripening gradually since then. Though a certain discovery of the absoluteness of God lies at the heart of all forms of religious life, these forms themselves are diversified. They vary and renew themselves endlessly as the history of the Church unfolds. What kind of religious life would Brother Charles embrace? It was for the Trappists he set off, but he shortly left the monastery of Our Lady of the Snows in France for a monastery in Akbes, Syria. Then he left the Trappists and turned up as a solitary servant to some Poor Clare nuns in Palestine. Next it was the Sahara where he was a priest, a hermit, and, in his own sort of way, a missionary. He saw himself mainly as everybody's brother, a humbly attentive brother, his ear all tuned to the poorest. In all these shifts should we read uncertainty, hesitation and instability? Is there on the contrary a real continuity which makes them all just steps along a path? In the letter to Henry de Castries already quoted, one sentence gives a clue to the underlying unity of his life:

> The Gospel showed me that the first commandment is to love God with all your heart and that everything had to be enfolded in love. Everyone knows that love's first effect is imitation. Therefore I was to enter the Order where I would find the most exact imitation of Jesus . . .

Yet isn't "imitating Jesus" the aim of any Christian life? And does there exist a congregation that doesn't propose to lead its members to the imitation of Jesus? What then is special to Brother Charles's case? Perhaps it is his discovery of the intensity of love where this desire for imitation is rooted: a very personal, one might say passionate love for Jesus. It is a moving discovery. Then, there is the fact that out of all the stages of Jesus' life and aspects of His mystery, it was the hidden life which would most inspire Brother Charles's meditation and prayer and so would most rouse his thirst for imitation. Because the gaze of his faith was flooded with the light of the hidden life of Jesus, he desired with all his might to live that hidden life. His vocation, as he often said, was not to imitate Jesus in his public life and preaching, but rather the hidden life of the poor and humble workman of Nazareth.

There is no doubt that his reborn faith was stimulated and strengthened from the very time of his conversion by the mystery of the Incarnation and the lowliness the Son of God took on Himself. He had heard Father Huvelin, his director, say in a sermon as if addressing Jesus, "You so took the last place that no one has ever been able to get it away from You."

Brother Charles would always say that these words had "indelibly engraved themselves" in his heart. The unthinkable humility of God touched him radically. And since he could not

> conceive of love without a need, a compelling need, to be alike, to resemble, and above all to share all the sorrows and difficulties and hardships of life,[1]

he would imitate Jesus in the humility and unobtrusiveness and all that made up his hidden life. He wrote to his cousin Madame de Bondy:

> My life's goal, as you know, is to imitate Jesus' hidden life at Nazareth as perfectly as it can be done, just as our dear St. Francis imitates His apostolic life.[2]

If he entered the Trappist Order, it was in search of this life: "It seemed to me that no one offered me this life better than the Trappists."

And he was to live several years in the monastery with a great inner peace, a peace he mentions in all his letters. But he feared for his poor and hidden life when he began to hear talk of reform in the Order. He wrote to a Trappist Father who was then in Rome for a general chapter:[3]

> We have come to the Monastery to find here the solitude, the poverty, the humble work and the penance that make our Order unique in the Church, the only one where those the Lord calls to follow Him in His hidden life at Nazareth find their place. If something is changed in this solitude, this poverty, this humble, menial and blessed work of the hands, and this penance of the kind St. Benedict prescribed for us and gave as heritage to St. Bernard, I would be inconsolable, for the Order would no longer be the one I entered with such happiness.[4]

Brother Charles was mistaken. The Trappist monastery and this "Nazareth," whose outlines were taking shape more and more in the depth of his being, were two different realities which only partially overlapped. It might be that God had led him "through" the Trappists so that he would receive from them a solid initiation into religious life as such, and a setting where his inner life would mature. Yet it was "toward" another life God was leading him. What he lived in the monastery was to leave a deep imprint on Brother Charles, but he would leave the Trappists, and would do so conscious of the continuity in his search. Later he was to write:

> The Trappists are definitely not for me. Why I left the monastery is why I entered it. The reasons are the same. I was not disloyal to an ideal that I was hoping to find there but didn't.[5]

What he was looking for and hoping for — what the Lord was writing in the depths of his heart — was this imitation out of love. He wanted to imitate Jesus in that very humble and hidden life of His at Nazareth. That was what gave his life its meaning and direction, pushing him onward from step to step. To his friend Duveyrier[6] he explained in April 1890:

> Why did I join the Trappists? That's what your dear friendship asks me to account for. It was out of love, out of sheer love. I love our Lord Jesus Christ, though with a heart that longs to love more and better, yet I still love Him and cannot bear to lead a life different from His, a pleasant, respectable life when His was the harshest and most despised there ever was. I don't want to travel through life in the first class when the One I love travelled in the last class.

And in his meditations he often stops to consider the bonds that, to his mind, are necessary and inescapable between imitation and love.

Let us imitate, imitate Jesus! Imitation is the daughter, the sister and the mother of love. Imitate Jesus so as to love Him more. Imitate Jesus because He commands us to and because to obey is to love. The first word Jesus says to His apostles is, "Come and see,"[7] that is, "follow and look," that is, "imitate and contemplate." The last thing He says to them is, "Follow me,"[8] that is, "imitate me." To imitate Jesus contains all perfection; to imitate Jesus contains divine love itself, in which all perfection consists, for Jesus loved God perfectly . . .

From the moment someone begins to love, he imitates and contemplates. Imitation and contemplation are a necessary and natural part of loving, for love leads to union, to the transformation of the one who loves into the beloved and his unification with the beloved. And imitation is the uniting of a being with another through resemblance.[9]

THREE

START SOMETHING NEW?

Hidden life in the footsteps of Jesus was an idea that took form slowly in Brother Charles. He tells us that he had

> glimpsed it and guessed at it while walking the streets of Nazareth that our Lord's feet had trod when He was a poor workman lost in lowliness and obscurity.[1]

It was during his first pilgrimage to the Holy Land in the winter of 1888-89. He was still the Viscount de Foucauld. He had believed he was going to find this life by joining the Trappists, but he later confided to his cousin Madame de Bondy,

> From the beginning I saw it wasn't there, but I kept hope that perhaps it might be and that I could lead this life I was looking for in the monastery.[1]

Thus it didn't take long for Brother Charles to start asking himself questions. Was the Trappist life the imitation of Jesus he felt he was called to? Yes or no, was he faithful to his vocation in following this monastic life that seemed to him further and further from his ideal? At first he was all alone with his thoughts. Then came the moment when his ideas were more definite and the inner force that was goading him became stronger. He had to open up to others.

He spoke to his prior. To Abbe Huvelin, he wrote.
Likewise to his cousin. The letters he sent them are of
great interest to us, for they are the first known
sketches of his conception. They reveal among other
things what Brother Charles was living interiorly at
that time. What he was living was an agonizing
question: ought he to leave the Trappists? Or was the
Lord giving him such thoughts merely that he might
give them up? To live the hidden life, to live the life of
Nazareth, did he have to found a new congregation?
Here are the letters themselves. They are from 1893;
the one addressed to Father Huvelin is dated
September 22:

> By decree of the Holy Father there have been some
> very happy modifications made in the Order. But
> these modifications, these improvements, aren't keep-
> ing the evil from growing. They will give more unity
> in the Order and somewhat keep the abbots from
> each doing as he pleases. The level of studies will be
> higher for the monks who are priests. But all this will
> only pull us ever farther away from poverty, humility
> and the lowly life of Nazareth I came to look for here.
> I'm infinitely far from having given up wanting them,
> and it fills me with grief to see our Lord leading that
> life alone while no one or no group in the Church is
> thinking of living it with Him today and sharing for
> His Love's sake and in His Love the happiness that
> was our Lady's and St. Joseph's. Wouldn't there be a
> way to form a little congregation to do that? We
> would live only from the work of our own hands, like
> our Lord, who didn't live by taking up collections or
> receiving offerings, nor from the work of foreigners
> hired as laborers while He merely supervised.
> Couldn't we find a few souls to follow our Lord that
> way, to follow him in *everything* He said, absolutely
> renouncing all property, collective as well as indi-
> vidual. Then we could forbid absolutely what our
> Lord forbids — lawsuits, grievances, disputes. We
> would make it our absolute duty to give alms: when

we have two habits, give one; when we have something to eat, give to those who don't, keeping nothing
for tomorrow.

We would follow all the examples of the Lord's
hidden life and all the counsels that came from His
lips. It would be a life of work and prayers. There
would not be two categories of monks the way there
are in the Trappists,[2] only one the way St. Benedict
wanted. But we would not have St. Benedict's complicated liturgy, only long silent prayer, the rosary
and the Holy Mass. Our liturgy closes the doors of
our monasteries to the Arabs and Turks and
Armenians and others of the country here. They are
good Catholics, but they don't know a word of our
languages, I so desire to see these little households of
fervent, hard-working life just like our Lord's get
started under His protection, with Mary and Joseph
watching over them, near all the missions of the
Middle East, which are so isolated. They would offer
a place of refuge for the native people whom God
calls to serve Him and love Him alone.

Is it all a dream, Father? Is it an illusion from the
devil or is it a thought or an invitation from the Lord?
If I knew it came from God I would start this very
minute, and not tomorrow, all the proceedings I need
to set out on this path. When I think about the thing I
find it perfect. To follow the example and the counsels of our Lord can only be praiseworthy. And
besides, it is what I've always been looking for. It was
only to find Him that I came to the monastery. This is
no new vocation for me; if such a gathering of souls
had existed a few years ago, you know I would have
run straight there. Since it doesn't exist and nothing
that comes close to it or replaces it exists, shouldn't I
try to get it started? And to get it started with the
desire to see it spread especially in Moslem countries,
and elsewhere too?

I repeat, when I look at the object I find it perfect.
But when I look at the subject this thought has come

to, and come to so ardently! The subject, the weak and wretched being, the sinner whom you know — I don't see in him the material God generally uses to do good things. He uses good materials to do good works. It's true that once I make a start, if the thought comes from God, He will be the one who makes it grow and He will quickly bring in souls capable of being the foundation stones of His house. In front of those souls I'll stay as naturally as can be in the nothingness that is my place. Another thing gives me courage to undertake a task so little suited to a sinner and to my wretchedness. Our Lord said that when someone has sinned greatly, he must love greatly.[3]

There it is, Father. Do you think it comes from God? It's your answer and your advice that I'll take for guide, as you know. A father is always a father and most of all you for me. You see how I need you. This thought has been too strong in me for the past two months to let me think I could keep silence about it with my confessor, Father Polycarp. I spoke to him two weeks ago, but with far fewer details than I'm doing now. He advised me to let the thought sleep for the moment and not do anything about it until the occasion comes up. That's what I was thinking of doing too, but the occasion will come in a little more than a year when the time for my solemn vows arrives. Perhaps the occasion will come even sooner, whenever it turns out that we have our next canonical visit. It seems to me hard to imagine keeping my thoughts about all this from the Visitor. For the moment I try not to think about it. But I hardly succeed. In any case I had to tell you about it, and now it's done.

A few days later on October 4, he wrote to Madame de Bondy:

I just wrote a long letter by the last post to Father Huvelin to tell him what I had told you. I gave him still more details. Seeing that it's not possible in the

Trappist monastery to lead the life of poverty, lowliness, renunciation in practice, humility, and even prayerfulness, I would say, the way our Lord lived at Nazareth. I've been wondering if our Lord had given me these desires so vividly for the sole purpose of having me sacrifice them to Him. Or perhaps since there is no congregation in the Church today that offers the chance to lead with Him this life that He led on earth, I wondered if it wouldn't be time to look for a few souls with whom the beginnings of such a little congregation could be formed. The aim would be to lead as exactly as possible our Lord's life, living only from the work of our hands and not soliciting gifts or accepting any that are offered. We would follow all His counsels to the letter, possessing nothing, giving to anyone who asks, claiming for nothing. We would deprive ourselves as much as possible, first to be more like our Lord and then, almost as importantly, to give Him as much as possible in the person of the poor. Add to the work a great deal of prayer, though not Office chanted in choir, which is an obstacle for the native peoples and helps little to lead to holiness those who have no education. We would form only small groups, little dovecotes like Carmelite monasteries. Monasteries of many almost necessarily take on a material size which is the enemy of lowliness and humility. We would spread everywhere, especially in non-Christian countries where no one goes. It would be so pleasant to increase the love of our Lord Jesus there and the number of His servants.

This is what I've been thinking about for two months or so. It was after the regular canonical visit last winter that the first ideas sprang up. But they only came to me from time to time. After I studied our new constitutions about two and a half months ago, the thoughts became more frequent and more decisive in form. Then it all became a desire strong enough to make me feel obliged about three weeks ago to speak to my confessor, Father Polycarp, about it. I asked him if it came from God or from the devil or from my imagination. He told me to think no more about it for the moment and wait for the occasion that God, if it all comes from Him, will know well how to provide. It seemed admirably wise to me and that is what I'm doing. I made a gift of my desires to God and I pray that He makes me think about it only as much as will be for His greater glory.

Thus a dream received its rough outlines. But for Brother Charles it was the beginning of a difficult period, "a time of afflictions." Little brothers and little sisters cannot pass indifferently over the fact that Brother Charles went through such a trial at the moment when he started talking openly about making a foundation. What was this trial? A painful inner conflict: the call of Nazareth resounds in him more and more, an irresistible force pulls him toward something else, another life, a foundation. Yet he wants obedience to his superiors, and his superiors tell him, "patience and waiting." In almost all the letters he wrote from Akbes, he kept speaking of the deep peace he was experiencing, but he would confess that this period "around Christmas 1893" was a time of great distress. Though he usually speaks little of his difficulties, he would admit to a Trappist monk a few years later:

> I had many interior difficulties, many anxieties, fears, darknesses. I desired to serve the Lord, I was afraid of offending Him, but I couldn't see clear. I was quite troubled. I put myself then under the protection of Our Lady of Perpetual Help, begging her to guide my steps as she guided those of the Child Jesus, and to lead me in all things so that I would give consolation to our Lord Jesus, console as much as I possibly could the Heart of Jesus who watches us and loves us.[4]

FOUR

DRAFTS FOR A RULE

Asking himself such questions, Brother Charles quickly would start to answer them. While he was waiting for permission to lead his "life of Nazareth," he wrote down his ideas to clarify how he conceived it. Thus it was that in 1896, before he had even left the monastery at Akbès, he composed a first rule for the "Congregation of the Little Brothers of Jesus." A few years later when he was in Palestine, he drafted the Constitutions and Rule for the "Hermits of the Sacred Heart." He went over those constitutions again in 1902, when he was at Beni-Abbès, and from that time on he spoke of "Little Brothers of the Sacred Heart of Jesus." He wrote a similar text for the "Little Sisters of the Sacred Heart of Jesus."

These were elaborate drafts, where he aimed not merely at giving a general direction and describing a spirit, but entered into the details of the daily schedule, the means of earning a living, the work, food, housing and clothes of the brothers to be. The weakness lies there. These rules bear the stamp of an ardent love and an immense desire for poverty and humility, with Jesus for an example, but the problem with them is that no one ever lived them. They were never put into practice by a real community. Father

Huvelin gave the first of these drafts a cool reception when Brother Charles consulted him. "Your Rule is absolutely impracticable. Whatever you do, don't found anything. Lead a new life, but don't attract companions for it."[1]

Later, when men and women would take up Brother Charles's conception after him, they would not be able to use, as they were, his constitutions and rules. Yet the rules he wrote are, in their way, very authentic expressions of the fundamental intuitions that were prompting their author.

By way of example, here are some articles from the Constitutions of the Little Brothers of the Sacred Heart of Jesus:

Preliminary Article: TO BRING ABOUT THE REIGN OF JESUS AND OF LOVE, that is the mission of the Little Brothers of the Sacred Heart of Jesus, as their name implies. They are to make Jesus and love reign in their hearts and around them. Their fraternities, consecrated to the Sacred Heart of Jesus, must, as He did, shine out over the earth and "kindle fire"[2] there. The Little Brothers of the Sacred Heart of Jesus have as their particular vocation to imitate the hidden life of our Lord at Nazareth, to adore night and day the Blessed Sacrament always exposed in their chapel, and to live in mission lands. Their aim is to glorify God by patterning their lives on the life of our Lord Jesus, by adoring the Holy Eucharist and by making holy non-Christian people by bringing the presence of the Blessed Sacrament among them, offering the divine Sacrifice of the mass and practicing the virtues of the Gospel.

Article I: IMITATION OF OUR BELOVED LORD JESUS. The Little Brothers of the Sacred Heart of Jesus will make it their continual concern to become more and more like our beloved Lord Jesus Christ. How much one imitates indicates how much one loves: "If anyone wants to serve Me, let him follow Me!"[3]

Article II: PERPETUAL ADORATION OF THE MOST BLESSED SACRAMENT. The Most Blessed Sacrament will always be exposed, night and day, in each fraternity (except for the three last days of Holy Week), and there will always be two Little Brothers before it in adoration.

Article III: THE LITTLE BROTHERS OF THE SACRED HEART IN NON-CHRISTIAN COUNTRIES. The Little Brothers of the Sacred Heart of Jesus must go and live especially in the non-Christian countries of mission territories. However, it is also permitted for them to found fraternities in Christian lands.

Article VI: HOLY POVERTY. The Little Brothers may possess nothing personally. They must live by the work of their hands, in a great poverty the way our Lord Jesus Christ did. Everything about them must be poor and worthy of "the Workman, the Son of Mary":[4] their buildings, furniture, clothes, food, chapel, in short, everything . . .

Article XXIV: CHARITY WITHIN THE FRATERNITY. The Brothers will constantly recall that they are "Little Brothers of Jesus," living with the Holy Family in their home at Nazareth, and they will have for one another the charity, the thoughts, the words and the actions that are fitting in so holy a place in the company of Jesus, Mary and Joseph.

Article XXV: HUMILITY WITHIN THE FRATERNITY. The Little Brothers of the Sacred Heart of Jesus will cultivate humility with special care. Humility must perfume their fraternities as it perfumed the home of Nazareth. They will remember Jesus "meek and humble of heart"[5] and "subject"[6] at Nazareth, who "humbled Himself and became obedient."[7] They will rival one another in obeying each time that it is not a duty to do otherwise. They will bear the name "Little Brothers" because they must "become as little as a little child"[8] out of humility.

Article XXX: CHARITY TOWARD PEOPLE OUTSIDE THE FRATERNITY (MATERIAL ASPECT): The Little Brothers of the Sacred Heart of Jesus will give alms, hospitality and medicines with an extreme charity to all who ask, as if giving to beloved brothers, whether they be Christians or non-Christians, good or bad. They will heap special attentions on the poor and unfortunate, who are the suffering members of Jesus, and on sinners and unbelievers, so that they can "conquer evil with good."[9] They will not be "respecters of persons,"[10] and unless someone's health requires otherwise, they will give to all their guests, to the poorest as to the richest, the same food, the same lodging or the same medical treatment. In everyone they will see only Jesus. Their brotherly charity toward everyone must shine like a beacon, and no one, be he a sinner or an unbeliever, should fail to know for far around that they are universal friends, universal brothers, who spend their whole lives praying for all men without exception and doing good to them. The fraternity should be known as a harbor, a refuge, where every human being, at whatever hour he comes, is invited, desired and welcomed, especially if he is poor and unfortunate. The fraternity must be what its name says: the house of the Sacred Heart of Jesus, of Divine Love shining on earth, of the burning Charity of the Savior of men.

Article XL: THE END OF THE EXILE. The Little Brothers of the Sacred Heart of Jesus, whose particular vocation is the imitation of our Lord Jesus Christ, will remember with thanksgiving each day that since they live in mission territory among non-Christians, they can rightly hope to imitate our Lord Jesus in His death as well as in His life, and they will be always ready to give their blood gladly for Jesus, their one love. To Him be praise, honor, glory and blessing, with the Father and the Holy Spirit, world without end, Amen.

Taken as a whole, the Rules Brother Charles wrote in order to prepare the way for founding a new form of religious life suggest several important observations.

First, some elements can be seen to be fundamental, like a backbone to his conception. The first articles above expressed them: 1. Imitation of Jesus at Nazareth; 2. Adoration of the Blessed Sacrament; 3. Implantation of the fraternities in non-Christian countries. Once Brother Charles had formulated these three elements clearly, he would hold to them unwaveringly, and they turn up in all his Rules, personal notes and letters when he talks about founding a congregation.

Besides these basic elements, the texts contain some very beautiful teachings, particularly about the spirit of charity, poverty and humility that he wanted to see in the little brothers and little sisters. The articles cited are illustrations.

Still, if you were to read these texts in their entirety, you would find side by side with this rich doctrine any number of scarcely practical instructions. There are details that vary from one text to another or are even contradicted — for example on whether they would wear a habit, what the ideal number of brothers per house would be, or even the form of the vows they would take. Clearly, on points like these Brother Charles kept on searching, and his rules would naturally have needed to be tested with use before they could take on a final form. But in what he wrote, it's not the details that count for us; we come looking for a certain spirit, and it can be found there.

It's also noteworthy that when Brother Charles organized his own personal life, he tried to base it on this Rule for the Little Brothers of the Sacred Heart of Jesus. Witness the examinations he made of his life and the resolutions he took at his yearly retreats. This doesn't mean that, living alone, he obliged himself to follow to the letter a Rule written for a community, but he regularly got his inspiration from it and set out for himself to follow it "as one follows a handbook," which would help him "in certain matters, to enter into the life at Nazareth."[11]

His whole life long Charles de Foucauld was to think about founding congregations. His whole life long he was to wait for companions. None would join him.[12] One of his dreams nonetheless did get started while he was still alive. It was not a congregation but a spiritual association for people in all walks of life who wanted to follow the Gospel more fully in the situation or state of life in which they already found themselves. For them he wrote the "Directory," or handbook, which is a sort of adaptation for lay people of what he had written for religious in his Rule. His aim was threefold: to bring to Christians of every walk of life, a life patterned on the Gospel, imitating Jesus as their model; to develop in them a devotion to the Eucharist and a sense that it is the sacrament of Love; and to open their eyes to non-Christian peoples so that they would realize that their life has apostolic meaning. He based what he says on the same Gospel values; exactly the same spirit is at the heart of it. The ideal he sets out for the lay people of the association:

> They will take for their rule to ask themselves in everything, what Jesus would think or say or do at their place, and then to do it. They will strive continually to become more and more like our Lord Jesus, taking for their model His life at Nazareth, which furnishes examples for all the walks of life.

The measure of imitation is the measure of Love. "If anyone wants to serve Me, let him follow Me."[13] "I have given you an example so that you may do as I have done for you."[14] "The disciple is not above his Master, but if he is perfect he will be like his Master."[15] (Directory, Article One)[16]

FIVE

NAZARETH, OR THE HIDDEN LIFE

Leaving the Trappist monastery was an important moment in Charles de Foucauld's path. Father Huvelin heard about the Father General's decision right away and wrote to his spiritual son:

> Yes, like you, my dear child, I see you in the East. I prefer Capernaum or Nazareth or some Franciscan monastery. Not in the monastery, only in the shadow of it. Just ask for their spiritual resources and live in poverty there at the threshold. That, my dear friend, is what I can see as a possibility.[1]

At the beginning of March, Brother Charles landed in the Holy Land. Looking for a place to settle, he turned toward Galilee. He knocked at several monastery doors; it was the Poor Clare Nuns of Nazareth who took him on as a handyman. On March 22 he wrote to Mme. de Bondy:

> Since the first Wednesday I got to Nazareth, I've been a hired man at the Poor Clares'. I serve the masses and the benedictions of the Blessed Sacrament. I sweep, I go on errands, in short I do whatever I'm told to. My work starts after the eight o'clock mass in the morning and is over at five o'clock, which is when they have benediction of the Blessed Sacrament at least every other day. On Sundays and holidays I have nothing to do and I can pray all day long . . .

I live in a shed outside the cloister wall . . . This is exactly the life I was looking for.

Exactly the life he was looking for. At first sight that means a life where he could provide for his needs with humble work and then be able to give himself to prayer. His needs, moreover, he knew how to reduce, and the jobs the sisters gave him were very simple and left him plenty of time to meditate and pray. Yes, he had the life he wanted, the life of Nazareth. But what did that really mean? The life of Nazareth, the hidden life — Jesus is the one who holds the secret of it. He is the one who lived it first, in that same little village in Galilee. If someone wants to live that life in His footsteps, mustn't he first discover it in Him? And Brother Charles, in long written meditations, questions the One he calls the Beloved:

My Jesus, who are so close to me, inspire me with what I ought to think of Your hidden life.

"He went down with them and came to Nazareth and was subject to them."[2] He went down. He plunged downward, He humbled Himself. It was a life of humility. God, You appear as a man. As a man You make Yourself the last of men. It was a life of lowliness down to the last of the last places. You went down with them to live in their life there, in the life of poor workmen living from their toil. Your life was like theirs, poverty and obscurity. They were obscure and You lived in the shadow of their obscurity. You went to Nazareth, little lost town hidden in the hills, where "nothing good ever came out of,"[3] as people said. It was seclusion far withdrawn from the world and its metropolises. And You lived that seclusion.

You were subject to them, subject as a son is to his father and to his mother. It was a life of submission, a son's submission. You obeyed in everything as a good son obeys. If a desire from Your parents wasn't in

accord with the divine vocation You had, You didn't
do it; You obeyed "God rather than men,"[4] as when
You stayed behind three days in Jerusalem. But
except for the times when the vocation You had
required You not to fulfill their wishes, You fulfilled
them in everything. You were the best of sons, and
therefore You not only obeyed the smallest of their
wishes but even anticipated them, doing everything
that could gratify them, cheer them, make their life
pleasant, trying with all Your heart to make them
happy. You were the model of sons, attentive in all
ways possible to Your parents, in the measure, of
course, that Your vocation allowed . . .

That is what Your life at Nazareth was — Your life
here, since I have the infinite happiness and incom-
parable grace to live in this dear Nazareth. Thank
you, thank you! Your life was that of a model son
living with a father and mother who were poor
working people. That was half of Your life, the earthly
half, while it sent out all over heaven a celestial
fragrance. That was the visible part; the invisible part
was Your life in God, contemplation at every
moment. You worked, You cheered Your parents,
You spoke to them of tender and holy things, You
prayed with them during the day. But how You also
prayed in the shadow and the solitude of the night,
how Your soul poured itself out in silence! Always,
always praying, You prayed at every moment. For to
pray means to be with God, and You are God. But
Your human soul prolonged that contemplation
during the nights, just as during the hours of the day
Your human soul would live its union with Your
divinity. Your life was such a continuous outpouring
in God, a continuous gaze toward God, a continuous
contemplation of God at every one of Your moments.[5]

Meditations like these Brother Charles wrote
many of. If you read this one carefully and analyze it
a little, you will discover, as Brother Charles discovered, three main aspects in the life of Nazareth,

though we must not force the text and have to remember that he was not the one who made this distinction in an explicit way. He sees first the lowliness of the Son of God who became man and revealed Himself in a humble and hard-working life. Then he looks at the Holy Family and the remarkable bonds that united them. And last he raises his eyes to the very deep union that joins the Father to each of the three, Jesus, Mary and Joseph, but in an altogether unique way to Jesus. It is a gaze of faith that he turns toward Nazareth, because Nazareth is a mystery of faith. If when he meditates he strives to enter into the details of the historical situations as Jesus actually lived them, he is seeking a great deal more than a sweet, touching story. Jesus' lowliness in that simple, modest life is the condition by which He lived the mystery of the Incarnation and revealed it to us. The poor workman our faith shows us, the Nazarean carpenter, is the Word made flesh. This inward gaze of his, turned toward the mystery of Jesus, is fundamental if we want to understand Brother Charles when he speaks to us of the hidden life. According to him, a "life of Nazareth" in imitation of Jesus requires two things: to enter the world of the dispossessed realistically and without compromise, and to focus one's heart in faith and love on seeking Jesus as He lives the mystery of Nazareth.

In the same way when Brother Charles turns his gaze on the Holy Family, he sees much more than an edifying household. He sees the reality of the grace that united the members, the charity that transfigured all their actions and all their relations because of their holiness. He is in wonder at the relations between them, matching the real dignity of their beings — the Son of God, His mother, and Joseph — and at the

same time matching the function that each one by
vocation had to fulfill in the family and in the village:
parent or child, husband or wife, head of the family,
worker, and so on. Often in his meditations and from
time to time in his letters, Brother Charles pauses over
these relations within the Holy Family. In the text just
quoted it is the submission and the obedience of the
Son he considers; elsewhere it is the work, the
humility, the constant prayer, the austerity and so on.
Above all, of course, he ponders their charity.

In this same text, the train of Brother Charles's
thought brings us to discover with him the "other
half" of the life of Nazareth, the "invisible side," as he
called it. This is the union with God, not only through
family prayer and external worship, but the intimate,
totally interior bond that joins the Father to the
hearts of each one of the three. It is a bond of thanksgiving, of praise, of petition — or to say it in a single
word, of adoration.

Truly indeed the life of Nazareth belongs to
Jesus' mystery. The only way to imitate it and enter
authentically into the life of Nazareth will always be
from within an intensified life of faith, hope and
charity. Yet though we live this imitation at the depth
of the divine life within us, it is no less true that the
actual way Jesus originally lived at Nazareth gives us
a model and a teaching. Brother Charles saw that.

> You put only three years, my God, into teaching truth
> to the world, founding Your Church and forming
> Your Apostles. But You considered that it was not
> too much to consecrate thirty years to preaching to
> men the example of humility, lowliness and the
> hidden life.[6]

In one page of his meditations, he was encouraging himself, and all those who are called to this

hidden life, to set themselves faithfully to learn at this school:

> Then let us stay with Him in the place He stayed for thirty years. Let us stay where He teaches us to be by His example, as long as He doesn't call us to a life of preaching the Gospel. Let us stay with Him in the humble house of Nazareth, working people who live by exercising a humble trade, poor and lowly people who live disregarded, obscure, hidden and prayerful in the solitude and seclusion, the silence, forgottenness and communion with God, that poverty helps us so much to obtain. Let us plunge into our Lord's lowliness, poverty and humble manual work. Love requires imitation. Then let us love and let us imitate. "The servant is not greater than his Master."[7] We must be as little as Jesus. Jesus tells us to follow Him, so do it. Share His life, His labors, His occupations, His humiliations, His poverty, His lowliness. Be workingmen, poor workingmen, disregarded along with Him.
>
> Let us be crowned with the same crown of contempt and disregard as was our Bridegroom. Let us imitate Him and be little brothers to Him. We must live like Him in everything. "I am the way, the truth and the life";[8] we must follow that way and live Jesus' life, doing His works which are truth. "I came to save the world"; our goal is the same. We too must work, though not to redeem mankind, to contribute to their salvation. Our means should be the same ones Jesus used; His means were not human wisdom surrounded by pomp and splendor and seated at the place of honor. He used the means of divine wisdom, hidden under the appearance of a poor man, a workingman who though he was wise and versed in understanding, was poor, despised and lowly because He had never studied at the schools of men but was known to them as someone who lived under their eyes by a menial work.[10]

In the school of the life of Nazareth, Brother Charles would discover and sketch out for others the broad lines of a new style of religious life. In the treasures he found as he meditated on Nazareth, we have noted three aspects shining like three beams of light from its mystery: the lowliness of Jesus, the living charity at the heart of the Holy Family's life together, and the contemplation of God. From this triple light comes three keys which show Brother Charles, and many others after him and through him, what the life of Nazareth is to be for them. Nazareth must mean: sharing the condition of the lowly, living together in a household of fraternal love, and giving oneself to God for the prayer of intercession and adoration.

Sharing the condition of the lowly comes first. At the school of Nazareth, He who lowered Himself reveals the world of the lowly; He who made Himself poor among the poor reveals the world of the poor, His privileged friends. At Nazareth, the God who became a man leads those who have made up their minds to live only for God to their fellows.

For as long as the Church has existed, countless people have chosen to serve the poor in the name of the Gospel, and done so in ways very different but each authentic. Many are the apostles like St. Francis, who set out on the roads to preach the Gospel as penniless as the Twelve had been; many are the groups that have wanted to recapture the poverty of holding all goods in common as the first Christian communities did; many are the works of mercy that have sprung up to relieve the sufferings of the needy, receiving each person and loving him as if he were Christ Himself. With Brother Charles it was rather Jesus' life at Nazareth that he contemplated with special attraction, and so it was the poverty of Nazareth that inspired him and that he wanted to reproduce in his life. The poverty of Nazareth means the ordinary condition of simple people, the poverty of the poor. It consists in having no choice but to live on little, in depending on a manual work that is usually toilsome and gives a low wage, often unjust and unreliable. The poverty of Nazareth also means the obscurity of those who are ignorant and ignored, the disregard and disdain in which people too often hold those they deem without money, learning or power.

When he wanted to be like the lowly, as literally as his Beloved had been, Brother Charles put manual work into his life. One must not think it was always easy for him. When he started at the monastery, he spoke of:

> . . . a lively yearning to stay in the reaping and the woodcutting up to my neck, and an extreme repugnance for all that might come between me and the lowest place that I've come here seeking, with the lowliness that I desire to plunge ever deeper into, following the example of our Lord.[11]

But he made some discoveries too:

> We are between the mowing and the reaping, and here work is really work. It is poverty and mortification . . . [12]

He even admitted a little naively:

> Here work has an important place. I like that. Not that I like working, but work is the handmaid of poverty and the imitation of our Lord. Work is what makes the monastery like Nazareth.[13]

And to his sister:

> Finished reaping the wheat day before yesterday. It's

peasants' work, a work infinitely good for the soul.
While it keeps the body busy, it leaves the soul free to
pray and to meditate. And then, this work — more
grueling than you think when you've never done it —
gives you such a compassion for the poor and such a
charitableness toward laborers. You really know the
price of a piece of bread when you see for yourself
how much toil it costs to earn it. You sympathize
deeply with the workingman when you share his
work . . . [14]

Brother Charles was neither a peasant nor a
worker. He had a great deal to learn. Besides, it can
seem that the word "lowliness" and the adjectives
"base" and "lowly" and "despised" come back often
when he speaks of manual work. Should we be put
off? Not if we remember his background. Among the
nobility, manual work was considered contemptible,
and Brother Charles speaks the way the people of the
class he came from thought. He grasped immediately
that manual work was an indispensable element for
the form of poverty his vocation required, that
manual work belonged to Nazareth; it was only
gradually afterwards that he discovered that the work
was, in itself, noble and worthy of respect. When he
wrote his handbook in 1911, not for religious but for
lay people who wanted to commit themselves to a
Gospel life-style, he told those among them whose
work was mainly intellectual:

. . . They must join to it at least a few minutes each
day spent in a humble, menial work in order to
become greater by imitating the "workman, the son
of Mary,"[15] in order to live a little something and
understand a little something of the Holy Gospel (for
one understands the Gospel not by hearing it but by
practicing it), and in order to teach those around
them the nobility and grandeur of manual work and
inspire them to love and respect it.[16]

Meanwhile, eager to have his religious congregations get started, he wrote in the constitutions he drafted:

> One of the fundamental points of the Congregation is that following the example of our Lord at Nazareth, it must live exclusively from its manual work.[17]

> The Little Brothers of the Sacred Heart must, like our Lord Jesus at Nazareth, live solely from the work of their hands.[18]

A glance at the life of Brother Charles shows that he himself wasn't always able to do as much manual work as he would have wanted to. Writing to Fr. Huvelin from Beni-Abbès, he examined his conscience:

> I thought it was the right thing to do these past days to make a slight modification in my life. (It's the fruit of my meditations since Easter.) Until now I've scarcely practiced manual work at Beni-Abbès for several reasons: first of all, I see material things and all that is not sheer adoration of the Beloved as so completely not worth zero that my hands fall as soon as I come from in front of the tabernacle. Secondly, because giving alms, caring for the sick, comings and goings, guests and visitors, the sacristy, letters and the housework that I'm the only one who can do take up so much time already that I would have none at all left for prayer at the foot of the altar or for reading if I start gardening or bricklaying, too.

> In spite of these reasons that have held my hands still for eighteen months, I've started working manually in small amounts but regularly since a few days ago, for the following reasons: 1. It's an essential part of the life of Nazareth. 2. It's an important part of the Rule I've set for myself for a long time. 3. Of itself it's a good example set continuously, and one of the most needed ones here. 4. It's a means to be side by side both with local people and with soldiers, and a

chance to speak to them of the Lord many times a day. 5. It's the conclusion that all my Eastertide meditations have led me to. 6. It's humble. 7. Each time I've devoted myself to manual work, it's brought good fruits for my soul and the souls of others.[19]

Later he would be taken up in linguistic studies, for he wanted to know the Tuaregs' language fluently in order to be closer to them, understand them deeply and prepare the way for their evangelization. But he would often say how much in a hurry he was to finish in order to give more time to manual work. And he was careful always to do at least some humble housekeeping job himself. But leaving aside the question of just what Brother Charles did in his own life, it is certain that he is at the origin of a new way of seeing Gospel-based poverty in relation with religious life. Quite certainly he himself didn't explore to the full the new track he had opened, but this path would lead brothers and sisters to choices heavy with consequences when they set out to follow his inspiration. It can even be said that though he never suspected it, his ideal of the life of Nazareth was to become a few decades later a fruitful light for religious life as a whole and even for lay Christian life in the Church of the century that was then just beginning.

Manual work, then, is an element of the life of Nazareth. For those who choose Nazareth, it will often be the best school and will always be a requirement for faithfulness. But it is not all there is to it.

Choosing the condition of the poor is more than work. It has many factors and includes the location of the fraternity, the type of housing, the kind of furniture, and all the rest. Brother Charles notes that a fraternity ought to be set up

> on the outskirts of town, where land is cheaper and where the poor live. The house will be built the way

the poor of the country build theirs, either in uncut stones or in planks, adobe, woven branches or whatever. Basically the only rule is to do what the poorest of the area do.[20]

The details are not very important. It is the mention of the kind of house the poor people of the given area have that is interesting. When Brother Charles wanted to describe Nazareth, he had always based it on what Jesus had or did. Now he came to take for his point of reference what the poor people of the place were able to have or to do.

This is the exterior, the framework. Now we need to penetrate into the heart of what Nazareth means. In Brother Charles's vision of the fraternities he will found, he sees them in the overflowing light he has received from contemplating the Holy Family,

whose life we continually strive to reproduce and whose company we believe that we are always in. Each one of our houses will be called a Nazareth.[20]

The wealth of graces that he pictures shining in the life Jesus, Mary and Joseph led together, serves as his model for the virtues he wants his brothers to have.

We are in the house of Nazareth beside the Virgin Mary and St. Joseph, clustered like little brothers around our big brother, Jesus, with us night and day in the Blessed Sacrament exposed. This thought is enough to show us the duties we owe one another. We must have for the others the thoughts, the words, and the actions that befit the household of Nazareth in the presence of the Virgin Mary and Saint Joseph and at the feet of Jesus who tells us, "Love one another as I have loved you. It is by this sign that men will recognize that you are my disciples."[21] We must love all with a fond, brotherly love in Jesus and for Jesus.[22]

When they practice humility, the brothers

will remember Jesus, "meek and humble of heart"[23] and "subject"[24] at Nazareth, the one who "humbled himself and became obedient."[25] [26]

And when he speaks of obedience, he imagines Jesus saying:

> I was subject to my parents for 30 years. Of course they were holy. But they were merely human and I am God. How could you, after you see Me so obedient for so long to those to whom I really owed no obedience, whose sovereign Master, Creator and Judge I was, refuse perfect obedience to those of whom your God has told you, "Whoever listens to them listens to Me."[27] [28]

Thus he pictures all the Christian virtues — charity, humility, justice and obedience as well as poverty, chastity and piety — in such a way that he comes to see in the Holy Family a community where all the virtues of the Gospel are resplendent. It stretches things too far to look at the Holy Family as a religious congregation, but they can well be seen as the first of all Christian communities.

In addition he sees this life at Nazareth, hidden though it may be, as a light that shines and instructs. He wants the largest number of his fraternities to be implanted in non-Christian countries. He imagines Jesus telling him from Nazareth:

> What do I show you here? I show you first of all that one can do good to people, a great deal of good, an infinite good, a divine good, without words, without sermons, without noise, in silence and by giving the example. The example of what? Of piety, of fulfilling lovingly one's duties toward God, of kindness toward everyone, of tender affection for those close by, of doing domestic duties with holiness, of poverty, work, lowliness, prayerfulness, withdrawal from the

public, the obscurity of a life hidden in God, a life of prayer, of penance, of seclusion wholly plunged into God and lost in Him.[29]

Nazareth is definitely a decisive light for Brother Charles. This is his vocation "identified so many times." He was to live out this ideal intensely even though he remained alone. Later, at a time when he knew that brothers would not be coming soon, he wrote in his diary:

Take as your aim the life of Nazareth in everything and for everything. Take it in its simplicity and its breadth and use your Rule only as a handbook to help you enter into this life at Nazareth in certain things. For example (until the Little Brothers and Little Sisters are duly established): no habit — like Jesus at Nazareth. No cloister — like Jesus at Nazareth. Don't live far from where anybody else does, but close to a town — like Jesus at Nazareth. No less than eight hours of work a day (manual or otherwise, but manual as much as possible) — like Jesus at Nazareth. No big landholdings, no big houses, no big expenditures, or even big alms, but extreme poverty in everything — like Jesus at Nazareth. To sum it up: in all things, Jesus at Nazareth. Make use of the Rule of the Little Brothers to help yourself lead this life, but just as a holy guidebook. Resolve not to follow it in anything that wouldn't help you imitate this life perfectly. Don't seek to organize or prepare the establishment of the Little Brothers of the Sacred Heart of Jesus. Live alone here as if you were always to be alone. If there are two or three of you, or several, live as if there would never be more. Pray like Jesus, and as much as Jesus. As He did, always give a very great place to prayer. As he did too, give a great place to manual work, which is not time taken from prayer, but time given to prayer. The time of manual work is a time of prayer. Faithfully recite each day the Breviary and the Rosary. Love Jesus with your whole heart and love your neighbor as yourself for

His sake. Your life of Nazareth can be led anywhere.
Lead it wherever it is most useful for your fellowmen.[30]

There is one last text which recapitulates everything this life of Nazareth is about. He is speaking of how a fraternity is to resemble the house of the Holy Family:

> Everything about it must be a portrait of their house.
> Everything must be a reminder of it — walls, furniture, work, clothing, food. All of them must proclaim: humility, poverty, lowliness, penance, obscurity, seclusion, silence, prayer, hidden life of Nazareth; proclaiming: charity, charity, charity, especially toward the little. Above all else proclaiming: faith, hope and love, a life plunged into Jesus, Mary and Joseph and lost there in imitation, contemplation and adoration of Jesus the beloved.[31]

This text, which begins with the walls and the furniture and rises to the life lost in contemplation, gives a beautiful overall vision of the life of Nazareth in its totality. When people make this life their own it becomes necessarily an echo of the mystery of Nazareth.

For religious to want to live an intense life of faith, hope and love, turned wholly toward the desire for contemplation, and at the same time a life embedded as deeply as it can be in the social condition of the poor, including their manual work, is probably the originality, the boldness, and, one might say, the challenge of what the fraternities have set out to do.

SIX

KNEELING BEFORE THE TABERNACLE

In the projected rules for religious life Brother Charles wrote, he always gave a great place to "the adoration of the Blessed Sacrament."

> The Most Blessed Sacrament will be exposed night and day in each fraternity. There will always be two Little Brothers before it in adoration.[1]

For himself he set quite a strict standard when he was at Nazareth, resolving:

> 1. To spend as long a time as I can (after I have fulfilled the other obligations You impose on me more bindingly) before the Blessed Sacrament. 2. To spend as long a time as I can (after I have fulfilled the other obligations You impose on me more bindingly) in prayer before You in my hermitage whenever I can't be before You in front of the tabernacle. Doesn't someone who loves put ahead of everything else (except his strict duties) the endeavor to be as much as possible in the presence of the Beloved? Unless of course something else would please the Beloved more, for we must seek His consolation, His good, His will before our own.[2]

One might wonder, when Brother Charles set himself to stay in prayer "as long a time as I can," as if he wanted to set an endurance record. What counts is to see, underneath, his deep desire to be close beside his Beloved and submit everything to His Will. His letters often bear witness to what was going on in the depths of his heart. Among many others, here is an example. Arriving for the first time at Beni-Abbes at the end of October 1901, he quickly built his chapel and wrote to Mme. de Bondy at the beginning of December:

> Since December 2nd the Blessed Sacrament has been in the little chapel that Jesus has made for Himself at Beni-Abbes. Thus I am now day and night in the delights of His company. How blessed I am. Pray that I may be to Jesus a loving and faithful companion.[3]

And because he always saw his fraternities set up with perpetual adoration of the Blessed Sacrament and solemn expositions and benedictions, he set to work eagerly until at the end of that same December he noted, again to his cousin:

> At Christmas we had the Blessed Sacrament exposed from midnight till 7 p.m.; on New Year's Day we'll have it from 7 a.m. till 7 p.m. How I thank God for this grace. I was far from hoping there would be enough men coming to pray to make this possible. Jesus has provided them. The good will and unexpected piety of the neglected soldiers here around allows me to give each evening without exception a reading and explanation of the Holy Gospel (I just can't get over it that they accept to come listen to me), and then the benediction of the Most Blessed Sacrament. After benediction there is a short evening prayer. This benediction, along with the holy mass, is a consolation and an immeasurable joy.[4]

These forms of solemn worship were to be his joy, and moreover they were exactly in line with the way the Christians of his time practiced their devotion

to the Eucharist and to the Sacred Heart. But in fact
for Brother Charles they wouldn't last long. After the
first months of his stay at Beni-Abbes he began to
travel through the Sahara and he ended up alone at
Tamanrasset, where he had no more possibility of
such liturgies.

Brother Charles never developed at length anywhere in his writings a theological approach to the
mystery of the Eucharist. A tabernacle with the
presence of the Blessed Sacrament was of capital
importance to him in a fraternity, and his life and
work are marked by an intense devotion to this
Sacrament. But the reason was simply that Jesus
Himself, in His personal being, had captivated
Brother Charles's gaze — with a special attraction for
His lowliness, let us repeat. The Church told him that
Jesus is mysteriously present in the Eucharistic Bread;
so he went to be with his Beloved there, with an
extremely simple and concrete faith. The tabernacle
was to be the privileged place for long hours of conversation with his Friend. He loved Jesus, and Jesus
was there. That was the simple logic of his faith.

> Since our Lord is there, what would I gain by going
> elsewhere? He is there, what more could I need?[5]

Or again, this meditation where the vivid realism
of his faith comes out:

> You are there, my Lord Jesus, in the Holy Eucharist.
> You are there three feet away from me in the taber-
> nacle! Your Body, Your Soul, Your humanity, Your
> divinity, Your whole entire being is there in its double
> nature. How close You are, my God, my Savior, my
> Jesus, my Brother, my Spouse, my Beloved. You
> were no closer[6] to our Lady all the nine months that
> she carried You in her womb than You are to me
> when You come to my lips in Communion. You were

no closer to our Lady and Saint Joseph in the stable
of Bethlehem, in the house at Nazareth, on the flight
into Egypt, and all throughout Your family life than
You are to me right now and so, so often in this
tabernacle. Mary Magdelene was no closer to You
when she sat at Your feet at Bethany than I am at the
foot of this altar. You were no closer to your apostles
when You were sitting in the midst of them than You
are to me now, my God! How blessed I am. How
blessed I am. To be alone in my room and commune
with You there in the silence of the night is sweet, my
Lord, and You are there as God, as well as by Your
grace. And yet to stay in my room when I could be
before the Blessed Sacrament would be as if Mary
Magdelene, when You came to Bethany, had left You
alone to go off to think about You by herself in her
room. To kiss the places You have sanctified in Your
mortal life, the stones of Gethsemane and Calvary,
the pavement of the Way of the Cross, the waves of
the Sea of Galilee, is an uplifting devotion, my God,
but to prefer that to Your tabernacle would mean to
leave the living Jesus who is beside me, leave Him
alone and go off by myself to venerate dead stones
where He isn't. It means leaving His divine company
and the room where He is to go kiss the floor of a
room where He was but is no longer. To leave the
tabernacle to go and venerate statues means to leave
Jesus alive and by me, and go to another room to
bow to His portrait.[7]

It is truly Jesus Himself whom Brother Charles
encounters in the Eucharistic presence, not just one of
the aspects of Christian belief, but Jesus in the totality
of His mystery. His faith is vibrantly alive. That is
why it is close to the tabernacle that he prefers to
meditate and pray, why installing a chapel and a
tabernacle goes hand in hand with founding a fraternity as he sees it, why in his vision of those who will
some day come to fill up those fraternities he already
calls them "adorers." He wants Jesus to be at the

heart of every fraternity and each little brother or
little sister to be very close to Jesus.

Thus he was bursting with joy each time he set up
a new tabernacle, as his diary shows when he noted
the events on a trip, and wrote on July 8, 1904:

> Stay at Amra. Today since we seem to be going to
> stay awhile longer, I had the happiness of placing for
> the first time in Tuareg territory the Reserved Sacra-
> ment in the tabernacle. A chapel of dried branches,
> topped with a wooden cross, was built; a tent pitched
> under it makes a canopy over the altar to protect it
> from dust. The altar and the Blessed Sacrament are
> under the tent. Sacred Heart of Jesus, thank you for
> this first tabernacle in the land of the Tuaregs. May it
> be the prelude of many others and the herald of the
> salvation of many souls. Sacred Heart of Jesus, shine
> out from within this tabernacle over the people who
> are all around You without knowing You. Enlighten,
> guide and give salvation to these souls that You love.
> Convert and make holy the Tuaregs, Morocco, the
> Sahara, those who do not believe, all mankind. Send
> holy men and women, many of them, to labor for
> the harvest among the Tuaregs, in the Sahara, in
> Morocco and wherever they are needed. Send holy
> Little Brothers and Little Sisters of the Sacred Heart
> if it is Your Will. Convert me, wretched as I am,
> Sacred Heart of Jesus. To You be the praise, the
> glory and the blessing forever and ever.

We might wonder at Brother Charles's eagerness
to multiply chapels and hermitages in Moslem lands
and the way he rejoices when he places the Sacred
Host in a new tabernacle there. He speaks as if he
were taking possession of a portion of the Kingdom in
the name of Jesus, as if this land now belonged to
Him and from there on His Reign would manifest
itself actively with the Eucharist shedding light all
around just by being there. The little brothers "will

make non-Christians holy by bringing the presence of the Blessed Sacrament among them," he had written in his rule.

Perhaps Brother Charles's formulas are naive, but his faith is not. He never thinks of a tabernacle without an adorer kneeling before it. It is the living faith of those who will be there to adore Jesus in the Blessed Sacrament that makes His presence a light for the people around.

> My work here is, alas, only a work of preparation, a first clearing of the ground. I start by bringing Jesus into the midst of them, Jesus in the Blessed Sacrament, Jesus descending each day in the Holy Sacrifice of the mass. And I bring into the midst of them a prayer, the prayer of the Holy Church, however wretched may be the one who offers it.[8]

SEVEN

FELLOWSHIP OF SHARING
WITH THE BELOVED

The "beloved" of course is Jesus. How many times Brother Charles gives Him this title. "Sharing" is also a word that comes often from his pen, and it seems to be one of the best suited to express something of the relationship that evolved between him and Jesus.

If you think of his long meditations and the hours he spent in prayer, with such a marked preference for praying in front of the Blessed Sacrament, you cannot help wanting to know something of the dialogue that passed between those two friends, Brother Charles and Jesus. The inner depths of anyone's prayer are a secret, naturally. No one can say what someone's union with God is like. But echoes of what is going on deep inside a heart often come up to the surface, through what the person writes, for example. We may look, then, for some such echoes in Brother Charles's meditations and letters and other writings.

Already the way he expressed himself in his correspondence even before he entered the monastery gives a hint of the fundamental direction his heart was taking. To his cousin he wrote in September 1889:

> Father Huvelin and I went over once more the reasons why I wanted to enter religious life: to keep company to our Lord as much as possible in His afflictions.[1]

In November of the same year, writing to the master of novices at Our Lady of the Snows Monastery to which he was on his way:

> I find that your Order is the one where monks live most fully the Christian life and the life of total union with our Lord. Union with our Lord means sharing all His sentiments, it means living His life.[2]

The expressions "keep company with the Lord," "total union," "share His sentiments and His life," are full of meaning and already reveal the spiritual traits of the Brother Charles we know. This desire for a fellowship of sharing with Jesus comes back very often. He tells himself he must "share His afflictions," "share His prayers," "share His thoughts and His feelings." His search for his vocation, he tells Jesus, had led him to look for

> a life where I can share completely Your lowliness, Your poverty, Your humble labors, Your forgottenness, Your obscurity.[3]

And he writes in the Constitutions of the Little Brothers of Jesus, version of 1896:

> If we must imitate with love the external life of our Lord and put our whole hearts into doing it, how much more must we make our souls a likeness of His, think His thoughts, share His desires, have all His sentiments, and make but one heart and one soul with Him.

So then, what Brother Charles was doing for

hours upon hours was trying to know Jesus better in order to reach a fellowship where he made his own everything he discovered in Him. In a letter to Father Huvelin he tells the very simple method he has for following Jesus step by step, from town to town, from event to event. He tells too the great inward joy it gives him:

> My soul is still the same, still in that gladness and joy at the feet of Jesus. I delight in this simplicity of life, with these long hours of such simple and solitary prayer and reading. I am speechless with wonder at the way God leads my soul. I see how good it is for me to be here and how much I needed it. I sink deep into this peace. I'm astonished to see that reading theology, far from distracting me from union with Jesus, makes me enter the more deeply into it. My inner life consists in being united with Jesus in the different periods of His life on earth. Until tomorrow I am at Bethlehem, tomorrow morning I will go to the Temple, tomorrow evening I will leave in the night for Egypt. I will be with the Holy Family on their journey until Ash Wednesday; then I will go out into the desert with our Lord. A month before the end of Lent, I'll go along to Bethany to raise Lazarus from the dead and to keep company to our Lord during the last days of His life. Then I'll keep company to the apostles until the Ascension and Pentecost. From Pentecost until Advent I work and pray at Nazareth with the Holy Family. That's how I spend my year. As much as possible I stay kneeling before the Blessed Sacrament. Jesus is there. I think of myself as being there between His holy parents, or like Magdalene seated at His feet at Bethany.[4]

This method is too simple-minded? Don't say that too quickly. In the first place Brother Charles wasn't teaching a method; he was just saying what he did and how he worked at it, with a child's simplicity perhaps. But he wasn't a child, and he worked at it with the

resolute tenacity of an iron-willed man. He wanted to
assimilate all Jesus' actions and gestures, all His
words and the inner attitudes of His heart. Of the
immense effort Brother Charles put forth, the hundreds of pages of meditations he left are a proof.
"Effort" is the right word, for he didn't accomplish it
all with his heart warm and uplifted and his feelings
flowing easily. He speaks of his joy sometimes, but he
also speaks of his difficulties. He wrote out his
meditations for the very reason that he had a hard
time meditating.

> When I left Rome, I didn't want to write any more.
> But I found myself in such a dryness, such an
> impossibility to pray, that I asked my director if I
> should go on not writing or if I should go back to my
> written meditations. He answered me, "Write out
> your meditations. It's a very good way of praying,
> and it's particularly useful for you since it serves to
> focus your thoughts."[5]

All he wanted was to encounter Jesus. It is
very important, then, to see the great place Brother
Charles gave, as he sought this encounter, to meditation on the Holy Scriptures and especially on the
Gospels. Here he found another Real Presence of
Jesus, as he had in the Eucharist, and he clung to it.
Sometimes he took each Gospel from beginning to
end; sometimes he leafed through them seeking out
the virtues Jesus had practiced or taught. Sometimes
it was the events celebrated in the feasts of the year;
sometimes, a kind of rule of life he put together from
Gospel phrases, thinking he would publish it as a
booklet called, "The Divine Model." He wanted to be
penetrated through and through with these texts,
because he wanted to be penetrated with Jesus.

It's remarkable, and revealing as well, that he

seems to have invented a custom of putting a Bible in his chapel near the Blessed Sacrament. What seems normal to us with today's revival of Biblical devotions, must have been rather rare in those days in the Catholic Church. If Brother Charles came often to be in the company of Jesus in the tabernacle, he sought Him with the same constancy by meditation on the Scriptures.

Thus throughout his days Brother Charles strove to be with Jesus. He kept company with Him, he worked alongside Him, he met people with Him. He bore in his heart the griefs that wounded Him and rejoiced in His joy. He strove to share His immense desires for the world's salvation; he wanted to be a "savior with Jesus." He prayed to the Father with Jesus; he praised and gave thanks and adored through Him.

It was a relentless effort, earnestly straining toward a fellowship of sharing with the One he loved. Sometimes his effort buckled under his helplessness, for his desire was too great. Then he waited for his Beloved to do more in the dialogue, while he merely offered himself. It was that way in this meditation of his on the death of Jesus:

Think in me, Lord, and let me not think. Speak in me and let me not be the one who speaks. Let it be rather You, my God.

My God, You loved me even that far, even unto death. Give thanks in me; as for myself I cannot thank You. All I can do is give myself to You without reserve, begging You to give thanks Yourself in me. Prostrate at the foot of Your cross, "I commend my soul into your hands," I beg You to give thanks in me and to accomplish in me what will glorify You the most, to do in me what will please You the most. I give myself to You, do with me what You will,

I give You my life. Make me die a martyr's death as
You did, if it is for Your greatest glory and Your will
for me, if that is the way I can most glorify You and
be most pleasing to You. I give You my body and
soul and all the moments of my life; do with them
what most pleases You and glorifies You. Accomplish in me Your will. My God, here is Your servant,
a slave prostrate at Your feet with tears and adoration. Glorify Yourself in him according to Your will.
He belongs to You both by justice and by love. Not
his will but Yours. May Your will be done in him.
Amen. Amen.[6]

Brother Charles calls his prayer an adoration and
often speaks of adoring the Blessed Sacrament. When
you read his writings, "communion" is another word
that comes to mind for his prayer. This communion
overflows from sacramental communion, illumines
his days and brings him to a fellowship with everything Jesus lived for him, while he gives back to Jesus
everything he is living himself. "Adoration" too is a
good word for Brother Charles's prayer. Beyond the
Eucharistic presence, it contains the whole mystery of
Jesus and adoration of all Brother Charles discovers
there of God and His work of salvation. With Jesus
he adores the Father and the Father's plan.

All this leads him sometimes to speak of his joy,
his happiness to know God's Happiness. Expressed as
it is, this sentiment is enough to indicate the soul of a
real contemplative. Thus his Eastertide meditation on
Psalm 2:

... You are happy for all eternity. You are happy and
that is all I need. You are happy and therefore I am
in bliss. You are happy and therefore I want for
nothing. You are happy, O my God, and I am
plunged in Joy. What matter where I am, what I shall
be, I am in bliss, my Lord and my God, because it is
You I love and not me. It is in You where my self-

love is planted. Since You are happy, why have I to think of myself or of the world? I lose myself in the contemplation of Your bless, O my Beloved. I forget myself, I lose myself in You, I see You happy in Heaven, happy in the tabernacle. Good or bad, whatever I may be, You are happy, O my Lord, and nothing can take Your happiness away from You. So therefore nothing can wrench away my happiness. I have only to look at You and tell myself over and over that You are happy. If I'm able I might stammer the Regina Caeli Laetare or tell the glorious mysteries on my rosary. Or else I will lose myself at Your feet in the joyful contemplation of the beatitude where You dwell and which my sins cannot take from You.[7]

No wonder he describes this as ideal in the Rules of the Little Brothers of Jesus:

We set ourselves to imitate constantly our beloved Lord Jesus so as to be His faithful likeness in all our inward and outward actions. In our prayers we will ask Him for His Spirit, the kindly Spirit that He promised us. In our daily meditations and our yearly retreat, we will reflect deeply on His words and examples so as to be by His grace so intimately steeped in His Spirit that we think His thoughts, speak His words, do His actions, as much as can be so. We will ask ourselves in all things what He would think or say or do in the circumstances we are in, what He would think or say or do in our place. And we will strive with all our hearts to reproduce lovingly in ourselves the features of our divine model.

We will try hard, first and foremost to imitate His interior virtues to make our soul like His soul, afire with the love of God, wholly occupied with seeking His glory alone, wholly obedient to His will, single-mindedly set on the imitation of His perfections, lost in His contemplation, seared like a holocaust by the fire of voluntary sufferings, aflame with love for mankind, made in the image of God. We must become like Him, totally good, gentle, tender and

merciful, true, humble, simple, courageous, chaste
and detached from everything. Likewise we will be
diligent in imitating His exterior works at all times:
His poverty, self-denial and prayerfulness, His love of
solitude, obscurity and lowliness, His infinite kindness toward souls, hearts and bodies, His life consecrated to love and to serve and to save. We will ever
recall that He consecrated Himself to the salvation of
mankind to the point that the name "Jesus" sums up
and signifies who He was, for it means savior. We will
imitate Him by making the salvation of men the work
of our lives.

We will live in our fraternity with our eyes fastened
on the sacred Eucharist as if we were at Nazareth with
our Lady and Saint Joseph, looking always toward
our elder brother Jesus and trying to be like Him in
everything, until we dissolve in Him in a oneness that
grows more perfect every day. Our love has an
unquenchable thirst for this oneness here below.

These are the words that conclude that same Rule:

Let Him live in us. Let Him pursue in us His hidden
life at Nazareth. Let Him continue in us His life of
charity for all; let Him prolong in us His life of
humility; let Him by our faithfulness in doing penance "make up in ourselves what is lacking to His
sufferings."[8] Let Him by our watching and praying
continue in us to "spend his nights in prayer to God;"[9]
let Him by our limitless love for God continue in us to
be plunged in the love of His Father. Let Him by our
constant cooperation with His grace glorify His
Father in us in a wondrous way, provided we make
all the instants of our lives instants of His life, all our
thoughts, words and actions no longer natural and
human ones but divine, not ours but those of Jesus.
Let us act so as to be able to say at every moment of
our existence, "I live, but it is no longer I who live but
Jesus who lives in me!"[10]

We can gather that the path Brother Charles

opened is a path toward contemplation, and the call to follow this path is an invitation to make room for fellowship and sharing with the Lord as He will choose.

In conclusion, think again of a detail in the way he died: while Brother Charles's body sank lifeless into the sand, some looters in his chapel were letting fall into the sand, too, the container with the sacred Eucharist. Is it exaggerated to see the hand of the Lord making a sign that Jesus had granted His friend's great desire for fellowship?

EIGHT

WHOEVER LISTENS TO YOU, LISTENS TO ME

By entering religious life, Charles de Foucauld committed himself to a life of obedience. With a temperament as willful and independent as his, that was no small matter. Twice in the past, rather than yield, he had handed in his resignation from the army. His cousin and his spiritual director, who knew him well, sometimes questioned him in their letters about the difficulties he might be having. He answered:

> It's above all temptations against obeying mentally. I have a hard time giving in on my opinion. That won't surprise you. And yet, that's a small thing. I don't receive with joy enough the manual jobs I'm given, and that is a great lack of love.[1]

Was it easier at Akbès? Perhaps for the first few months:

> You ask what I think of submitting my judgment to obedience? I haven't thought four times about it since I left Our Lady of the Snows. I think you've been praying for me a lot.[2]

Yet he wrote to his cousin:

> How right you are when you speak to me sometimes about obedience. Speak to me often about it; if you

knew how much I need it! You do know. You know
me and you know too that if obedience is often or at
least sometimes difficult for me toward my superiors,
it's easy toward you. You know I listen to you. I
usually have hardly any trouble with obeying in
specific cases, but when I'm given orders leading to
something that doesn't seem desirable, for myself at
least I'm violently tempted to lack confidence in my
superiors. The devil is always there looking for a way
to turn everything to his advantage. This mistrust is
not always something new to me, as you know.[3]

Nothing extraordinary in that. All who have
tried to live obedience will find it familiar. In fact
Brother Marie Albéric put all the strength of his will
into obeying and mastering his independence of personality. What can amaze us perhaps is that Dom
Louis Gonzaga, his prior, was able to say of him, "In
all the force of the word, this is a holy monk. His
prayerfulness, his mortification and his obedience
know no bounds."[4]

When, yearning for a greater imitation of Jesus,
Brother Marie Albéric felt impelled toward a different life from the monastery's, his anxiety came from
not knowing any more what he should do. To obey
those who were telling him to forget it all or to wait —
his Trappist superiors and Father Huvelin himself —
was what he ought to do and what he wanted at all
costs. But what about obeying the voice inside him?
Was that not equally the voice of God? He knew well
that he could not judge with certainty about this voice
except through his superiors. But his superiors were
hesitant, and their reason was precisely that they
knew Brother Charles. They were afraid that his ideas
would give him a way to dodge a life of obedience and
claim back his independence. Inspiration or illusion?
It wasn't easy to discern, and so his superiors waited

and tested and put delays. Meanwhile within him the pressure kept growing.

> My thirst to exchange my religious status for that of a simple domestic servant or a simple day laborer at some monastery is becoming more and more intense. What I aspire to is always the same, but stronger every day. Every day I see better that I'm not at the right place here, every day I desire more to throw myself into the last and lowliest place, following in the footsteps of our Lord.[5]

Time went by and the hour for his decision now approached.

> On February 2, my five years of temporary vows will be over. On this date I will have either to make my solemn vows that I do not want to make under any circumstances, or else ask for a dispensation and leave.[6]

Whether or not they thought it would change his mind or put him in touch with persons who could enlighten him, his hard-put superiors in any case gave him a change of scene and sent him to the Abbey of Staweli in Algeria. He stayed there a few weeks. Then he was sent to Rome to study. He obeyed. In the fall of 1896, he started classes at the Gregorian University. The tension inside him was great. More than ever he wanted to be somewhere else, but more than ever he wanted to be under obedience. So he surrendered his will completely, accepting anything. And it was when he had sunk his heart completely into obedience that unexpectedly the Superior General of the Trappists gave him an answer that let him go his way: his vocation, they recognized, was not the monastery. The following day he wrote to Father Jerome, a monk at Staweli:

> I've just had to exercise a lot of obedience this week.

And now obedience is still what I have to exercise, and courage as well. And so I need your prayers . . .

I've been asking for three and a half years to change from the rank of a choir monk to a domestic servant, either in the Order or in another religious order somewhere in the East. I think that is my vocation: to descend. With the permission of my confessor I had made that request. My superiors had given me the order, before they would grant it, to go and spend some time at Staweli. When I got there, to my great surprise, I received the order to go to Rome, and here where I supposed that I would have to wait a long time still for the permission I've been sighing after for so long, when I thought I would be here for another two and a half years, without my having asked anything or mentioned anything, our good and worthy Most Reverend Father General took me, examined my sentiments, reflected on my vocation, prayed, called together his Council, and all of them in a unanimous vote declared that it's God's will for me to follow this path of lowliness, poverty and humble manual work, the workman's life of Nazareth that He Himself has been indicating to me for so long. Consequently all the doors are open for me to stop being a choir monk and descend to the rank of a domestic servant.

I received this news yesterday from the mouth of our good and worthy Father General, whose kindnesses for me touch me so deeply. But the time when I needed obedience was before he made his decision. I had promised the Lord that I would do whatever Reverend Father would tell me after he had examined my vocation as he was about to do, and whatever my confessor would say. Thus if they had told me, "You will make your solemn vows in ten days," and then again, "You will receive Holy Orders," I would have obeyed with joy, sure that I would have been doing the will of God. For since I sought solely the will of God and had superiors who sought solely the will of God too, it was impossible that God not make His will known to us. And still now, I'm in God's hands and under obedience.

I've asked where I should go when I leave here a few days from now. It will be the East. To what house I haven't the slightest idea. The Lord will show me by the voice of my director.[7]

There at the inmost depth of self-denial, all the doors were opened to him, "while I was praying merely that Father General might do Your will."

God had led his superiors to this decision that they hardly seemed to lean toward, and Brother Marie Albéric marvelled. His trust in the mediation of superiors and directors for knowing the will of God was fortified by it. Since he wanted to continue to obey, he put himself totally into the hands of Father Huvelin. For every important decision he would write to him; he submitted to him all his projects. The words of Jesus, "Whoever listens to you, listens to me,"[8] come back almost like a refrain in his correspondence with his director.

This teaching he gives us by his life is surely the best. But later on Brother Charles was often to speak of obedience. Is his doctrine original? We don't think so. Expressed through his meditations or taught directly in some letters he wrote giving advice to others, his conception of obedience is thoroughly traditional. But the thing is to sense how, throughout his writings he sees obedience wholly as a matter of Love. It is the Beloved you obey; it is His will you want to know so as to do it. When you love you cannot help wanting to do what pleases the one you love. When Brother Charles speaks of obedience, love comes through all over.

Obedience is the measure of love. Let us have a perfect obedience so as to have a perfect love.[9]

The depth to which his conception of obedience brought him can be seen in this meditation on Abraham in Genesis 22:

> Love is to obey You, to obey You with just such promptness and just such faith in something that breaks your heart and staggers your mind and overturns all the ideas you had. Love is the immediate and absolute sacrifice of the dearest thing you had, of your will . . . the sacrifice of your only son, the most cherished object your heart contains.

> Love means to exchange all goods against all sorrows for the sake of the Lord. That is what you do so wonderfully when you jump up in the middle of the night to go and sacrifice your son, holy Abraham. That is what You will do, O Son of God, when You come on earth to live such a life and die such a death. My God, make me do likewise, according to Your most holy will. Holy Abraham and holy Isaac, pray for me.[10]

And here is another of his letters to his friend Father Jerome:

> This is what I wish you: resemble Jesus, imitate Him, be His likeness. I send you a little picture I drew with the caption, "What is life good for if not to imitate Jesus?" The first degree of imitation is obedience and the last degree too. Imitation says everything, and obedience says everything. Obedience was Jesus' life at every moment: "My food is to do the will of my Father."[11]

> May it be our life too, and thus we will imitate perfectly our Beloved. For our part we know through the voice of our superiors and directors the will of God, that Jesus for His part contemplated directly in the Divinity.[12]

Finally, here are some glimpses into the deepest dispositions of Brother Charles's heart:

I want absolutely nothing but what He wants and I desire absolutely nothing but the perfect accomplishment of His will.[13]

Everything you may decide will be received with joy, gratitude and blessing, and will be accomplished to the letter.[14]

The more I forage through my soul, the more I see only one will there: to do what the Lord wants of me, whatever it may be. To do what will please Him most, glorify Him best, whatever contains the most love and will bring me to love Him most. I just want to glorify Him the most I can.[15]

I have always stayed within this obedience throughout my religious life.[16]

After Brother Charles settled in the Sahara, he as often as not had to make his decisions alone of necessity. He would write, describe his situation in detail and ask his director or bishop for advice or permissions. The mail took weeks, sometimes months, to get there, and the answers often arrived too late, or the situations changed in the meantime. Brother Charles was thus quite alone to make decisions, as he was alone in all other ways. That changed nothing in the inward dispositions he had always had. He had wanted, for example, to leave for Tamanrasset in 1903, but did not have time to receive back from his bishop a letter giving him permission before the convoy was to leave. And so he added to his request:

If I afterwards receive an order from you not to stay in the south, I won't stay. I am not leaving so quickly out of lack of obedience to you, but because the most perfect obedience (and it's part of its perfection) includes taking initiatives in certain cases. If I leave without hesitating, it is because I am ready to come back without hesitating. As easily as I am leaving, I would come back.

If he repeated so often those words, "Whoever listens to you listens to me," encouraging himself and encouraging others, it was because he knew well the struggle he had to wage to become a man of obedience. The testimonies that come through his own letters or that his monastic superiors give, show us the result.

NINE

THE UNIVERSAL BROTHER

While in France for his ordination, Brother Charles asked himself if he should return to Palestine or settle elsewhere. He made his choice as follows:

> Wouldn't it be better to go to the Holy Land? No. A single soul is worth more than all the Holy Land and the rest of inanimate creation along with it. I must go not where the ground is most sanctified but where the souls are in the greatest need.[1]

A few years later, writing to one of his correspondents, a priest in Paris, he explained how this thought had led him to Beni-Abbès. After telling what his life had been like in Palestine at the Poor Clares' convent, he continues:

> . . . The retreats before I was ordained a deacon and then a priest, showed me that I was to lead this life of Nazareth, my vocation, not in the Holy Land I loved so much, but among the souls that were most sick, the sheep that were most lost and most forsaken. The divine banquet, whose minister I was about to become, had to be offered not to brothers and relatives and rich neighbors, but to the lamest, the blindest, the poorest, the most forgotten of souls, who most lacked for priests. When I was young, I had travelled through Algeria and Morocco. In Morocco, the size of France and with ten million inhabitants, not a

single priest outside the capitals. In the Algerian Sahara, seven or eight times the size of France and more populated than used to be thought, a dozen missionaries. No people seemed more forgotten to me than these. I asked for and was given permission to settle in the Algerian Sahara.[2]

This principle which he followed for his own choices, he wanted to be that of the Little Brothers:

The Little Brothers of the Sacred Heart of Jesus will consider as one of their basic rules, not only to set up the large majority of their fraternities in non-Christian territory of mission lands, but still more to choose as the places for their foundations the countries that are most forsaken, most forgotten, hardest to reach, most lacking in laborers of the Gospel. Their particular vocation is to go like the Divine Shepherd[3] in search of the "most lost of the sheep," and like the Divine Physician[4] to the aid of "the sickest of souls."[5]

He had, then, when he settled in the Sahara, a very decided missionary desire. The method he intended to use was very clear too: he would live the life of Nazareth, the hidden life. He explained to his cousin:

Coming back to the subject of Morocco, you guess that if I've come and put myself here at Beni-Abbès on the border, what I really have in mind is to do everything possible that the Gospel might penetrate there. I won't stop being a silent contemplative monk; that's my vocation. I won't go preach like St. Francis' first holy disciples; that's not my vocation, and it doesn't seem to me the means to make Jesus known and loved. I'll try to found a monastic colony of poor monks who adore the Blessed Sacrament at Beni-Abbes and then to found others nearer and nearer to Morocco. I'll prepare the way for that from a distance by getting to know Moroccans here, and giving them the inclination to accept me in their country by receiving them here with brotherly hospitality.[6]

Hospitality was one of Brother Charles's concerns when he drafted his projects for congregations. He still thought very much along the lines of religious life as he had known it at the Trappists', and it was only gradually that he got over planning for cloister and strict daily schedules and other such things as they had been at the monastery. But deep within him he had an intuition that his foundations would be much more open and accessible. He called them "fraternities," to mean that anyone who came there was to be received as a brother. The idea of hospitality is spread throughout his constitutions and rules; the simplest is to cite here a few passages from the Rule of the Little Brothers of the Sacred Heart (1901):

"You have only one Father, who is in heaven."[7] "God created man in His image."[8] "Whatever you do to the least of these, you do it to me."[9] These three verses are enough to show the Little Brothers their duty of immense charity extended without exception to all men, who are all "children of God," "in the image of God," and "members of Jesus." Faithful to their name and to the heart and cross they wear on their habit as a symbol of infinite Love, and to their divine model, they will carry all men in their hearts as did their Brother and Bridegroom Jesus, who died for the whole human race.

With any soul they meet, they will keep ever before their eyes their mission toward every person. This mission is to bring salvation. In every person, good or bad, friend or enemy, benefactor or persecutor, Christian or unbeliever, they will see a soul to be saved. They will make themselves "all things to all men, in order to gain them all."[10] They will hate evil, but this hatred will never keep them from loving people. They will carry everyone in their hearts, even the most wicked, taking Jesus' Heart for their model; they will be friends to one and all in order to be saviors to one and all. Disciples, imitators and members of Jesus, their life has the same goal as His, to save all men for God's sake. Their life must, like His, be summed up and expressed in one word: Jesus, "savior." They will not bring salvation by preaching but by the offering of the Holy Sacrifice and the presence of the Eucharist. They will bring salvation by practicing virtue, by penance and prayer, and by a charity that sees in every human being only a member of Jesus to lavish with favors and lead to heaven. This is the immense and all-embracing charity that must shine out from the Fraternity as it shone from the Sacred Heart of Jesus.

To make Jesus and charity reign: this is the mission of the Little Brothers of the Sacred Heart of Jesus, as their name says. They must make Jesus and His charity reign in their hearts and around them. Their Fraternities, consecrated to the Sacred Heart of Jesus, must as He did shine out on earth and kindle fire there. "I have come to light a fire on earth, and what will I but that it be kindled?"[11] Everyone far and wide around us must understand the meaning of our name and the heart they see on our habits. Everyone must regard our Fraternities as harbors of Love, "the home of the Sacred Heart of Jesus, of Divine Love shining on earth, of burning charity, of the Savior of mankind."

These fervent exhortations in general terms go along with numerous practical directives that are not all out of date:

The Little Brothers of the Sacred Heart give hospitality, alms, and in case of sickness, medicines and treatments, to anyone who asks, Christian or non-Christian, known or unknown, friend or foe, good or bad . . .

We do not run a hospice, but we give hospitality . . .

Our guests, the poor, the sick, all are welcomed with reverent respect, with holy joy and with the attentive care due to the members of our Lord Jesus . . .

The fraternity is the dwelling of the Good Shepherd . . .

Rarely did the rich cross the threshold of the holy house at Nazareth; it was the poor who came there with confidence. We must make it so that the poor come with confidence to the fraternity. Though we should receive the rich with great love, we should not try to get their visits or wait for them. But let us wait for the poor and arrange everything so that we can give them a good welcome.

And in a letter to his friend:

This is evangelization, not by words, but by brotherly charity for one and all.[12]

Those were his desires and intentions. Once Brother Charles got to Beni-Abbès, he had to pass to action. He did so with ardor. He did his utmost to make himself really available to everyone. He wanted everyone to feel at ease in his fraternity, and reflected on just what attitude he needed to have toward the local inhabitants, toward slaves, toward beggars, toward nomads — as well as toward soldiers and officers who came to the fraternity too. He wanted to welcome everybody, but to remain vigilant that the poor be the best received. During his times of retreat he would think over point by point what he had written earlier in his projects. He noted his errors and made resolutions. You can feel from these resolutions the concrete difficulties he had already met in loving and serving the poor whom he had given hospitality to as brothers. This time we are no longer on the level of intentions and plans:

Wash the linen of the poor. Clean their room regularly. As much as possible do it myself. As much as possible myself, and not somebody else, do the lowest of the housework — clean the toilets and the rooms the local people use. Do whatever is "Service" and resembles Jesus by being among the disciples "as one who serves."[13]

Bear with the presence of the bad, as long as their wrongdoing doesn't corrupt the others . . . Every person alive, however bad he may be, is a "child of God" . . .

Overcome this natural severity I feel toward sinners and my repulsion, and replace it by compassion, concern, zeal and assiduous attentions given to their souls.[14]

He had to overcome a good deal in himself to welcome everyone, really everyone. It wasn't so easy in the particulars, person by person and day by day, to "see Jesus in every human being," as he set himself to do. He probably struggled a long time on this point, his whole life long most likely. A good intention is not enough to make you become poor among the poor in reality. He wrote to his bishop describing his way of acting with each person — guests, the elderly, the sick, the soldiers — and he added:

To have a precise idea of my life, you have to know that people knock at my door at least ten times an hour, rather more than less. Poor people, sick, passers-by, so many that though I have great peace, I have great activity along with it.[15]

Over and over, he turned to his model, Jesus. Thinking about His miracles, he would observe Jesus' way of responding to people and write meditations like this one:

It is not enough to do all the good one can to all men, for their bodies or for their souls, because all are members of Jesus. One must go further and do this good with the tender eagerness, the graciousness, the alacrity that Jesus shows.[16]

Before all else, that is what his apostolate was to be:

> My apostolate must be an apostolate of goodness.
> Seeing me, people should say, "Since this man is so
> good, his religion must be good." If someone asks
> why I am meek and good, I should say, "Because I am
> the servant of One who is much better than I. If you
> knew how good my Master Jesus is." I wish I could
> be good enough that people would say, "If that is
> what the servant is like, what must the Master be!"[17]

And it was a great joy for him when he noticed that
the nomads and the oasis-dwellers understood that his
hermitage was a "khawa," which meant "fraternity."

> I want all the population — Christians, Moslems,
> Jews and polytheists — to get used to thinking of me
> as their brother, their "universal" brother. They've
> started calling my house "the fraternity", and that
> gives me a lot of pleasure.[18]

Universal charity thus meant for Brother Charles
an open door, a welcoming heart, a mind alert to
know and understand the others the way they were. It
didn't require travelling up and down the world. Once
he had settled in the Sahara, he didn't leave except for
a trip or two to France. When he wanted little
brothers with universal hearts, "friends to one and all
in order to be saviors to one and all," what he
pictured in them was a spirit of brotherhood open as
wide as possible to their neighbors, as his was.

> From 4:30 in the morning till 8:30 at night, I am
> always talking and receiving people: slaves, the poor,
> the sick, soldiers, travellers, the curious . . .[19]

> People here are starting to call my house La Khawa,
> meaning that the poor have a brother here, and not
> only the poor, but everyone.[20]

Who more than Jesus had had a heart universally

open to all? Yet the earthly paths He travelled were quite limited. So Brother Charles concentrated on seeing with Jesus' eyes those who came to his door. But from the beginning he dreamed that his little brothers would be spread all over the world. Jesus' disciples were sent out after Him to all the nations.

Those who later took up his path among nomads of the Sahara understood, after a few years of trial and error, that to be faithful to his message their fraternities would have to spread among all the poor of the world. Today they are widely dispersed, even to places that till now have been difficult for the Church to reach — among nomad groups and isolated handfuls of people, across difficult borders and in de-Christianized settings. The fraternities now reach from Alaska to New Guinea, and from Chile to Japan.

Living closely bound to fraternities all over the world and the realities of their situations, has deepened the universality of each little brother's and little sister's heart in a very concrete way. This dispersion all over the world also means vocations from many diverse origins. The fraternities then, little households of three or four, can translate into their everyday life what it means to be universal. It is a very demanding work of love. The brothers or sisters come from very different backgrounds and temperaments and experiences, from countries that have been colonized and those that have done the colonizing, from peoples at war with one another. The path of unity can only pass through suffering and the bearing of sorrow; real unity is something Jesus alone makes possible. It is this humble attempt to love realistically without barriers, on the strength of Jesus' love, that makes them a leaven of peace where they are hidden.

TEN

GO TO THE MOST FORSAKEN

To be consecrated to the poorest and the most forgotten was another of Brother Charles's very strong desires. And among the miseries and poverties of men, the condition of not knowing Jesus and the message of His Gospel seemed to him one of the greatest. Thus he always wanted his fraternities to be founded, not exclusively, but by priority in non-Christian countries. Remember how the mere fact that he was the only priest who could go there weighed heavily as an argument for choosing Beni-Abbes for his first fraternity. He thought he could find there those "most forsaken" he had made up his mind to give himself to, and he dreamed of being able to strike up some relations with Morocco, whose inhabitants seemed to him more forsaken still, at least as far as their possibilities of receiving the Gospel were concerned. Thus it was at Beni-Abbes that he settled down to live his hidden life as a little brother, and rapidly this hidden life of Nazareth began to give off its light.

Yet Brother Charles would stay at Beni-Abbes only a short time. What happened? While he was at Beni-Abbes, his life seemed full of activities. He bought land. He got some soldiers to help with the building, and soon he had a chapel, a hermitage, a guest room. His bishop even told him, "You build too much," modest as his hermitage was. He had a garden and date palms. "Five or six hard-working brothers in seven or eight years could make a magnificent palm plantation," surely enough to feed the community of brothers he hoped for so much, and never was to see. The village was fairly large, "a hundred and thirty hearths." There were many nomads around, and it was a stopping place for caravans. A great many visits, then, for Brother Charles — he received "sixty or a hundred visitors a day." He gave out large amounts of alms; later he would resolve, "not to give as much in alms as I did at Beni-Abbès, as if I were a monastery when I am alone." People respected him. Moved to revolt by the wretched condition of the slaves, he undertook by correspondence a campaign of protest with the authorities, which fell short. He succeeded, however, in ransoming a few young slaves, until he ran out of money.

The garrison at Beni-Abbès then counted two or three hundred Europeans, so of course there were Christians among them, and he found listeners for his few short explanations of the Gospel, worshippers to pray with him, servers for his masses, helpers and even a few friends. Careful not to make too much of his relations with the officers, he spent time with them nonetheless. He was held in esteem. And no matter how much he had to do, he knew how to find time to spend long hours of prayer in his chapel.

All that was excellent, and at the same time remained very humble. Yet what happened next made it seem as if, perhaps, in the eyes of God what Brother Charles was doing was still too big, too imposing, as if he had too much support all around there and was too much in view, as if these weren't the most destitute, whom he was meant for. Across the events that shaped his course little by little, the Lord was to lead him to other poor people, other forsaken people whom he hadn't thought of before. It was among them that he would live his Nazareth. Among them Brother Charles would find his greatest solitude, his greatest poverty and his greatest abandonment.

It happened like this. A colonel was setting out on a peaceful visit to regions that had recently surrendered. The colonel was Laperrine, a long-time friend. He invited Brother Charles to come with him. Brother Charles was dreaming of pressing westward toward his Morocco, and the route proposed to him led south and east. What matter. The former explorer wavered however, hesitating to set out on a journey. Out of character?

> I have absolutely no stomach for it. I shudder, I'm ashamed to say, at the thought of leaving Beni-Abbes, the calm at the foot of the altar, and throwing myself back into travelling, for which I have an excessive horror. My mind shows me lots of draw-backs: the tabernacle at Beni-Abbès would be left empty . . .[1]

He would leave nevertheless in January 1904, and the journey lasted several months. Wasn't he the only priest authorized to go to those zones, the only person who could go there in the name of Jesus? And so he went, as he told Henri de Castries, "from campsite to campsite, trying to get people used to my presence, to gain their trust and their friendship."[2] A year later he came back to Beni-Abbès just for a few months, for he was soon to leave again for "those parts of the Father's field that are so forsaken," and this time he would settle far from everything at Tamanrasset among the Tuareg tribe.

He faced a serious problem however. Ought he to renounce celebrating Mass? As long as he was travelling, he had always found among the soldiers a Christian to attend. In those times the liturgical discipline was strict. To settle at Tamanrasset meant to remain most of the time without mass, since he would be the only Christian for hundreds of miles around. Would he make up his mind to do it, when the Eucharist was so important for him?

> Being the only priest who can go to the Hoggar, while many can celebrate the Holy Sacrifice, I think it is better that I go in spite of everything to the Hoggar.

> Formerly I used to see the infinite worth of the Holy Sacrifice on one hand, and the finite value of all that is not God on the other, and so I would always let everything go for the sake of the celebration of mass. But there must be something missing in this line of reasoning, for since the Apostles, the greatest saints have on certain occasions sacrificed the possibility of celebrating mass to works of spiritual charity, journeys or other.[3]

Staying on at Tamanrasset since July 1907, he could only rarely celebrate mass if some Frenchman was passing through. The permission he asked for from Rome for celebrating his mass alone took a long time coming, and a certain sadness shows through in his letters.

> December 8, Feast of the Immaculate Conception, No mass . . . Christmas, tonight no mass. Until the last minute I kept hoping someone would come, but no one did, neither a Christian traveller nor a soldier nor permission to celebrate mass alone. It has been three months, more than three months, since I got any letters. May the Will of the Beloved be blessed in all things.[4]

At last on January 31, 1908, the permission

came. From then on he could celebrate mass alone. His joy exploded. But it was rumored that an expedition for Morocco was under preparation. He had dreamed of Morocco for so long; he loved the country and he had friends there from the time of his exploration. His heart leaped, and he was ready to move on again. He was barely getting over a long and serious illness, but he paid no attention. Hadn't he written to his bishop in 1903:

> I am wretched without limit, and yet, search as I may within myself, I can find no other desire than this one: Adveniat regnum tuum. Sanctificetur nomen tuum. You ask if I am ready to go elsewhere than Beni-Abbes for the spreading of the Gospel. For it, I am ready to go to the ends of the world and live till the Last Judgment.[5]

Would this rumor of an expedition be a call from the Lord, then? No, it would only give him reason to write to Bishop Guérin afterwards:

> If I had been called for the expedition to Morocco, I would have left the very same day. I would have done 60 miles to get there in time. But no one said a thing to me.[6]

And so he stayed. "The ends of the earth," had turned out to be for Brother Charles this village of Tamanrasset, a paltry "twenty shacks scattered over two miles," though the nomads around were numerous. Solitude. It was there that he would have his Nazareth to live. These were the people who would mean for him the most forgotten.

Such a steadfast resolution as his to go toward the most forsaken, such a readiness to pick up and move again and again, such a willingness to accept any hardships, even spiritual ones, can only strike us as extraordinary. It is remarkable that his spirit of

faith should have guided him so well in his choices
and led him to risk all his securities, even the most
legitimate of them, to go out toward men. The love
for Jesus that was always on his lips, and his attach-
ment to the Eucharist, didn't serve him as a pretext to
keep people away from him, but rather impelled him
toward his brothers. Isn't that the best guarantee that
his love was authentic?

> I think that there is no passage of the Gospel that has
> made a deeper impression on me or changed my life
> more than this one: "Whatever you do to one of these
> little ones, you do it to Me."[7] If we think of it, that
> these are the words of Uncreated Truth, words from
> the mouth that said, "This is my body . . . This is my
> blood," then how forcefully we are impelled to seek
> Jesus and love Him in the "little ones," bringing all
> our spiritual means for the conversion of souls and all
> our material means for the relief of temporal troubles.[8]

Scattered across the world to follow Brother
Charles in their fraternities, the brothers and sisters
learn the geography of wretchedness. Each people has
its own brands. Where people live who are poorer,
more backward, more looked down upon, more
outcast, more isolated, there is likely to be a place for
a fraternity. There are fraternities in shantytowns, as
you may well guess, but there are also fraternities
travelling with gypsy caravans or circuses, or pitching
their tents among nomads in Africa. There are sisters
in prison side by side with prisoners. There are sisters
on a sampan in Hong Kong and brothers shipping out
on trawlers or freighters. These are extreme among
the situations of brothers and sisters, yet difficult and
unexpected as they may be, it is there that the Lord
invites some to lead their religious life.

ELEVEN

CRY THE GOSPEL WITH YOUR WHOLE LIFE

Zeal for souls: the Brothers' rule is to see in every human being a soul to save, and to put all their energies into the salvation of souls as did their Beloved, until the name "Savior" sums up their lives as it expressed His.[1]

Jesus wanted His name "Savior" to show the meaning of the work of His life: the salvation of souls. The work of our life must be in imitation of our one and only Model, the salvation of souls.[2]

These two texts are strikingly similar. The first one comes from the Rule of the Little Brothers which Brother Charles drafted in 1901 and revised the next year. The second one is an extract from the little notebook he started the year of his death. They frame the years of his presence in the Sahara. This thought of being "Savior with Jesus" comes back to Brother Charles over and over and is one of his key ideas. It is only normal, for his Beloved, the One he has set himself to imitate, is the One who gave His life for the world, and Brother Charles is eager to share His thoughts and desires. So, with the eyes of his faith fixed on Jesus, he writes resolutions like this one:

Be all things to all men with a single desire at heart: to give souls JESUS.[3]

And when he examines his conscience he asks:

> Do I carry all men deep enough in my heart, like
> Jesus' Sacred Heart?[4]

It is normal too that someone who spent so many
hours in prayer should have given a large place to
intercession:

> For quite some time, and more every day, I haven't
> been able to get my mind off Morocco with its ten
> million inhabitants, not one of them a Christian. So
> many people so totally neglected. Not one priest, not
> one missionary. In the ports where there are Spanish
> consulates, there are chaplains, and that's all. In the
> interior, in this country the size of France, not one
> altar, not one priest or religious. Christmas night will
> go by without a mass there, without one tongue or
> one heart pronouncing the name of Jesus. People are
> right to say, pray for France which is headed for
> perdition. But however grievous the upheavals in
> France may be, what are they beside this night of
> bereavement in Morocco? I think of them day and
> night and I pray. My prayers before the tabernacle
> and at mass go out to them. But not to them only. I
> don't forget the others. Still, my special thought, my
> particular prayer, goes mainly toward them, more
> and more toward them. This thought doesn't leave
> me.[5]

Brother Charles's desire to consecrate his life to
the salvation of men is clearly intense. It is time to
ask, will he use mostly, or solely, spiritual and interior
means like prayer and self-sacrifice, the way Carthusians do or the way St. Thérèse of Lisieux did, which
earned her the title of patroness of the missions
though she never left her convent? Or does he plan to
be directly an agent of evangelization? If so, how?
Here are a few more texts, first of all the lines which
follow the excerpt from the Rule just quoted. The

little brothers, he writes:

> must be "saviors" by the presence of the Blessed
> Sacrament and the offering of the Holy Sacrifice, by
> the imitation of Jesus' virtues, by penance and prayer,
> by kindness and charity. Charity must shine out from
> the fraternities as it shines from the Heart of Jesus.
> They will be zealous in administering the sacraments
> of Penance and the Eucharist within the fraternity,
> and in getting Christians from outside the fraternity
> to make retreats there if they ask to. They will make it
> their concern to procure for the people around them
> the religious assistance they lack, promoting the
> establishment of parishes or of houses of religious
> congregations. They will be sure to keep part of their
> chapel for the faithful. "I came to light fire on the
> earth, and what will I, if not that it be kindled?"[6]

Thus Brother Charles counts among his means a
radiant charity, with a certain exchange of services
and aid. Later he will call it "the apostolate of
goodness." He also sees a genuine ministry to be
exercised toward Christians who would come to the
fraternity looking for spiritual support. And he
speaks, though rather vaguely, of "promoting the
establishment of parishes, etc." for the sake of the
peoples around.

What he rejects, in the way of means, is clearer,
as in this other text of the same Rule:

> In truth we do not collatorate in the glorification of
> God, the work of our Lord or the salvation of souls
> by oral preaching of the Gospel. Nevertheless, we
> collaborate efficaciously by bringing among people
> Jesus as He is present in the Holy Eucharist, Jesus
> offered in the Holy Sacrifice, the Gospel virtues, and
> the Charity of Jesus' Heart which we strive to put into
> practice. Not having received from God a vocation
> for the word, we sanctify people and preach to them
> in silence the way the Blessed Virgin sanctified and

preached to John the Baptist and his household when she brought our Lord there and practiced His virtues.

Brother Charles loves the Visitation for the very reason that Mary, still absorbed in the words that have been spoken to her and the mystery that is being accomplished in her, carries Jesus to her cousin's house, going there simply to do her a humble service such as any mother can do for another. In the apostolate Brother Charles wants for his fraternities there is an element, then, of silent but light-giving presence in the midst of people. And he indicates that when he speaks of giving light he is thinking of a radiance from an intense union with God much more than of exterior activities.

> One day I would say to My Apostles, "Preach," and I would give them their mission and trace out its rules. Here in the Visitation, I speak to other souls, I speak to all those who possess Me and live a hidden life. I tell them, sanctify souls by bringing Me among them in silence. I say, "All of you, all of you, work for the sanctification of the world. Work for it as My Mother did, without words, in silence. Go and establish your pious retreats in the midst of those who do not know Me. Bring Me among them by setting up an Altar and a Tabernacle there. Bring them the Gospel not by the preaching of the mouth but by the preaching of example, not by proclaiming it but by living it. Bring Me to the world, hidden, silent souls, the way Mary brought Me to John.[7]

But the texts just quoted were written at the beginning of Brother Charles's quest, when he had thought a lot about his ideal but hadn't yet had time to put it into practice. His notions are still cloudy about the way he's going to fulfill his vocation. This much he knows: he is the "old sinner who from the morrow of his conversion has been powerfully at-

tracted by Jesus to lead His hidden life of Nazareth."[8]
This much too he knows: if he has come to the
Sahara, it is in the name of the Church's mission to
spread the Gospel to the whole world. What he has
yet to discover is how he will fit together his life
of Nazareth with a sense nevertheless of having a
mission. One can remark that he will always be a bit
at a loss to identify himself in traditional categories. Is
he a missionary? Sometimes he gives himself this title
and sometimes he rejects it. "Isolated missionaries
like me are becoming fewer and fewer," he wrote to a
French author in 1916, but to his Bishop in 1907 he
had said, "I am a monk and not a missionary, made
for silence and not for words." Elsewhere he calls
himself by the double title "missionary monk." The
basic problem was that this life of Nazareth of his is
something original, and there were no categories that
really contained it. When he referred to other distinc-
tions, they too quite traditional ones, he classed
himself among contemplatives rather than religious of
the active life, though without any overtones of a
claim to superiority:

> Who would dare say the contemplative life is more
> perfect than the active life, or the other way around,
> since Jesus led both kinds of life: One thing only is
> truly perfect, to do the will of God.[9]

In any case he avoided regular preaching. This
was a real choice on his part. He didn't do it primarily
because such discretion was particularly well suited to
a Moslem country. It was an inner requirement of his
vocation. He rejected likewise medical or educational
services that would require any but the simplest of
means, whereas those would have been the sort of
projects he could easily have undertaken in Islamic
surroundings. And as we have seen when he went

from Beni-Abbès to Tamanrasset, his faithfulness to his own quest impelled him to reduce his activities and his distributions of alms.

On the other hand, he didn't refuse whatever modest things any neighbor can do for another: favors, little helpful services, bits of advice. It didn't take him long to understand that cloister had to be a very relative thing in a house of Nazareth, and the monastic wall he had planned to build in Beni-Abbes never got further than a little row of stones. A home like the one at Nazareth had to be welcoming and easy to come to.

Missionary: Brother Charles is one in a sense. As much as any apostle among non-Christians he bears in the depths of his heart a responsibility for the spreading of the message of salvation. He carries it in his prayer, in his work and in his concerns; but since he is a man of the hidden life he realizes that he can use as his means of operation only such things as are fitting to a life of obscurity. More exactly, it is the hidden life itself which is his own way of working for evangelization — a humble and unobtrusive way, a path of extreme poverty as to its outward means. It is the path of little services rendered, neighborly help, friendly advice, hospitality (a thing so important to desert dwellers); his evangelization consists in sharing the way of life of those around him, in bearing in common hardships and sufferings, in patience and the slow process of getting used to one another, in friendship.

Meditating on the Gospel, Brother Charles sometimes identified three dimensions to the life that Jesus had led and that people were to imitate: the hidden life, the life of solitude in the desert, and the life of spreading the Gospel and public preaching.

The lives of mission or of solitude are for you, as they were for Him, merely the exception. Practice them each time His Will clearly indicates it for you. As soon as it is no longer indicated, go back into the life of Nazareth.[10]

Gradually things become clearer for him. Except for a few times of retreat, he is not made for complete solitude. Whatever ministry comes his way — for example bringing the sacraments to sick or wounded soldiers — he will accomplish zealously, and do it well, for he knows that the imperatives of charity rank ahead of the requirements of his personal vocation. But as soon as he can, he will get back to his life of Nazareth. He moves like a free man, and has all the more assurance going about acts that are exceptional for him, the surer he becomes as to what his usual life should be like: a daily life of just being among people and as much as he can being like one of them. His normal duty means simply to be available for a multitude of little services, for receiving visitors, for listening and speaking. Conversation with people individually or in little groups belongs to the life of Nazareth. Brother Charles always pays extreme attention to the words he can say to help and enlighten those who come to see him in his hermitage or whom he himself goes to visit:

> I should speak more than I do about Jesus to those around me . . . I should devote a certain amount of time each day — a sacred time — to evangelizing the men who do work for me, my permanent guests, and the guests who are passing through . . .[11]

He wrote that at Beni-Abbès just after he got there. Later he became wiser and more realistic about how to go about it, but he kept the same preoccupation.

Stick to natural theology when I speak, but keep in mind the aim of explaining Christian tenets . . .[12]

No use to speak to them directly of our Lord. That would drive them away. Win their confidence, make friends with them, do them little services, give them good advice, build up bonds of friendship, encourage them discreetly to follow their natural religious intuitions, prove to them that Christians love them.[13]

I render service where I can, I try to show that I care. Whenever the time seems right I speak about religious tenets that come naturally, God's commandments, His love, union to His will, loving one's neighbor. A few people, only a few, question me seriously about religious matters. When I give advice, I stay within natural religious intuitions, emphasize avoiding sin, praying each evening and examining their consciences, telling God their contrition and their intention of charity.[14]

Shortly before his death he wrote the same things to René Bazin, the French author who would one day write his first biography:

You have to get Moslems to accept you, become for them the trustworthy friend they turn to when in doubt or sorrow, whose love and wisdom and justice they count on absolutely. As our fellowship gets deeper established, I speak more about God, always, or nearly always just between the two of us. I speak briefly, giving each one only what he's ready for: to avoid sin, to tell God he loves Him with his whole heart, to want to be wholly sorry for his sins, the two great commandments of loving God and our neighbor, to examine his conscience, to meditate on preparing for death and judgment, the duty of creatures to be mindful of God, etc. I pay attention to what each one is capable of and move forward slowly and carefully.[15]

Thus he would help the friends, to whom he

couldn't yet transmit his faith, to direct their hearts toward the One God, speaking to them only of the beliefs they held in common. All that was measured to the one he was talking to. The chief of the Tuaregs was then Moussa ag Amastane. He and Brother Charles saw each other often, and there was a great trust between them. The notebook where Brother Charles marked down the things he wanted to remember to speak of with Moussa is still preserved; the subject was as well how to love God as how to promote the social evolution of his people, the attitude to have toward courtesans, toward French authorities or toward slaves. His aim with Moussa as with everyone he talked to was to meet each one where he was and encourage him to take the step forward he was capable of.

Naturally, he saw well that the Tuaregs had needs that he, the man of Nazareth, couldn't answer. Attentive to all aspects of life, he thought of the women and girls of the tribe. Since he had no little sisters, he wrote letters to various congregations of nuns asking them to make foundations in the Hoggar. He already investigated the possible places for them to live and consulted the authorities, both Tuareg and French. He pictured the possibilities of getting Christian lay people to come. He also spoke up to the officers, giving them suggestions on better government, and took the defense of Tuaregs whose rights were violated.

He remained very faithful to the spirit of Nazareth, but what he saw of the needs of the Tuaregs and the experience he acquired as he put himself at their service, brought developments to his thought about the congregation he never gave up desiring to found. A letter he wrote in 1911 to a Trappist, Father

Antonin, allows us to follow the change. He chose his words with care, for he was writing this letter to be shown to possible candidates for the little brothers. Here are a few passages:

> You ask me what my life is like. It's the life of a missionary monk founded on three fundamental ideas; imitating the hidden life of JESUS at Nazareth, adoring the Blessed Sacrament exposed, and settling among the most forsaken of non-Christian people, doing all that can be done for their conversion.

> I am alone and have been for six years. If the Lord should give me brothers, seeing the vast expanses of unbelieving territories to be converted, it would be better for the salvation of souls to divide ourselves into small groups of three or four, as many groups as possible, instead of forming bigger monasteries . . .

> The life is a monastic one: fasting and plain food, no wine, great poverty, manual work like the poor and the peasants, but in moderation.

> . . . According to the aptitudes of the brothers, the needs, and what he believes to be God's will, the Superior of each little group of three or four will assign each of his brothers either to full-time manual work or else to some manual work and some apostolic work. Apostolic work as I've done it up until now and as I conceive of it consists in individual conversations with non-Christians (and on occasion with Christians) . . .

> I see these outposts, these hermitages of three or four missionary monks, as a vanguard meant to prepare the way for other religious organized more like secular clergy, and to yield the place to them when the ground has been cleared.

> . . . We mustn't think of bringing in European foods here. That would be a costly luxury. We must live on what the people of the country live on: wheat, dates, and milk products. For our clothes and our quarters,

you find nothing resembling the tidy garments or houses of France. But they are very like what must have been the clothes and the poor dwelling of Jesus at Nazareth.[16]

We must also mention the considerable linguistic work Brother Charles achieved to get a grasp on the Tamashaq language the Tuaregs spoke. He thought of himself, of course, as working for the future, laying the groundwork for those who would succeed him in bringing the Gospel. But he also knew that he could not enter into deep relationship with the people unless he knew thoroughly their language and their culture. You can sense that for him it was a matter of respect for this people. Admittedly Brother Charles was fairly gifted for such a task. He compiled dictionaries, complete and abridged, collected poems and, naturally, translated the Gospel. Hadn't he, when he was young, achieved for mere scientific purposes and for his own personal success a remarkable hold on the culture of another people when he was exploring Morocco? He must have done it well enough to have managed to live nearly a year among this people without his nationality being detected. Now his desire to be the messenger of Jesus among the Tuaregs could hardly allow him to do less.

In the end Brother Charles appears as a man completely given, someone who no longer belongs to himself, but rather to the people of the Hoggar, and who wills to give his life for their redemption.

I cannot say I desire death. I used to wish for it. Now I see so much good to do, so many souls without a shepherd, that I mainly want to do a little good and work a little for the redemption of these poor souls. But God loves them more than I do, and He has no need of me. His will be done.[17]

All that, one may judge very good and generous but not exceptional. How many missionaries have done such things, and done still more. One can even find it most surprising that Brother Charles got such small results. He observes it himself:

> I haven't made a single conversion to speak of in the seven years I've been here. Two baptisms, but God knows what those baptized souls are and what they will become: a baby boy the White Fathers are bringing up, and God knows how he'll turn out, and a poor old blind woman — what was going on in her poor head and how real is her conversion? As significant conversions, it comes to zero. And I would say something even sadder: the farther I go, the more I think it's not the thing to do to try to make isolated conversions (except in special cases) for the time being.[18]

And in fact he didn't make any. The day of his death Brother Charles could have written the same things: no baptisms, no conversions, no churches founded, no fraternities, not a single companion to go on after him, not even any works that were going to last. And yet we claim that his life is in the mainstream of the Church's missionary vitality. Mission means the call the Church has received to carry to the whole world both the message of salvation in Jesus Christ and that salvation's reality. "Go and make disciples of all nations, baptizing them in the name of the Father and the Son and the Holy Spirit."[19] True enough, this mission is achieved through works, and on that score we have perhaps little to learn from Brother Charles who accomplished so little. But the mission is achieved first and foremost by persons. And maybe it can be said that the Holy Spirit, whose task it is to tell us things again and again throughout the ages, has made certain Gospel qualities stand out vividly in the life of Brother Charles. The Spirit led him to ways of being that the Church has always known about perhaps, but that he revitalized, brought close and made almost tangible for our world of today, so much so that even in the annals of the Church's mission this devotee of the hidden life has turned out to play a role of great importance. Quite obviously, he never suspected it. All he wanted was to follow Jesus and to be faithful to his personal vocation, but his life is a real message, and this message contains an apostolic dimension. As such it first affects the fraternities born after his death, who have chosen to be his followers. But the scope of the message is much broader still, and will apply to all those who work for the evangelization of the world today.

The message always comes down to Nazareth. But now we can express it in a somewhat different way from before. Brother Charles started by fixing his eyes on Jesus, and was drawn that way into His hidden life. But the more he looked at Jesus, he learned — and showed us too — a new way of looking at people and the situations they live in. This is where the interest for the apostolic worker comes in.

Brother Charles entered into the humble realities of the hidden life and into manual work for the sake of imitating Jesus. He discovered that these realities were great and beautiful and meaningful, and that they made up the life of the vast majority of human beings. In a world dominated by the pursuit of efficacity, organization and maximum production, and yet a world that is beginning to perceive the limits of its systems and programs, Brother Charles proclaims to us the value of humble people and humble things. He helps us remember that when the Word of God became man, He became poor.

To become poor meant for the Son of God much more than adopting a situation of hardships and sacrifice. It meant to be taught by human reality. In the human nature that He took on concretely, the flesh He made His own, Jesus learned by experience what it is to be a man. He learned everything from us: poverty and work, hunger, thirst and weariness, family and solitude, fraternity, friendship and betrayal, obscurity and notice, joy and its exhilarations, heaviness, anguish and death. He learned all there is of our condition, with the exception of sin. That is what the path of the Incarnation meant. It was with respect that the Savior approached those He was coming to redeem. He began by sharing, making His own and feeling for Himself the same afflictions He was coming to deliver them from.

> To save us, God came to us, mingled with us, lived with us in the closest, most familiar of contact, from the Annunciation to the Ascension. For the salvation of souls, He continues to come to us to mingle with us, to live with us in the closest of contact, every day and at any hour in the Holy Eucharist. Therefore, we must, in order to work for the salvation of souls, go to them, mingle with them, and live with them in close and familiar contact.[20]

Brother Charles tells the little brothers and little sisters they must strive to be "Saviors with Jesus." He is instructing them to follow this same path of the Incarnation, to approach people by being taught by the other, taught by another people and another way of life, striving to make their own the new people's riches and their poverty, their language, culture and traditions, their conditions of life and sufferings, their struggles perhaps and their hopes most certainly. This adaptation naturally will remain partial, but must be whole-hearted. Before even looking at the needs and afflictions of the other, to heal and relieve, they are to see first the other as a person, someone, to know and share with. This is the kind of attentiveness Brother Charles meant by a silent presence among people.

Brother Charles would never have pretended to say that all should restrict themselves to the hidden life. Jesus Himself left Nazareth, gathered crowds, preached and healed. But perhaps it is worthwhile that there be some in the Church who have this special vocation to recall what Jesus did for so many years at Nazareth, and to recall as well that even in His apostolic life and on the cross, Christ always remained Jesus of Nazareth. Is it not up to every apostle to cultivate the qualities of heart that make him more and more like a man of Nazareth?

This is what Brother Charles's life has to say to messengers of the Gospel. He himself never elaborated on it, of course, in theological terms. It is an existential message from a life that reminds us the path by which, from Bethlehem to Nazareth to the cross, Jesus made Himself fully ours to save us. It was wholly realistic when the Word of God took on the features of man, the features of the poor.

To be sure, one could spend a lot of time going over Brother Charles's apostolic activities and analyzing what he did and didn't do, his motives, his evolution, etc. There is still work to be done for us to explore what we know of him. But we are convinced the essential of what he has to teach us is no other than what we have said already: he is for all who work to spread the Gospel a living lesson in how to approach their brothers and sisters.

Besides this essential point, for those who study

his life, one aspect or another sometimes takes hold of them more powerfully though not exclusively: that deep and silent presence of his, for example, or his will to give a welcome to everyone, his hospitality, or his very simplified way of working to spread the Gospel message. In fact, this is more or less what happened at the foundation of the various congregations born of his spirit. Each congregation has a slightly different approach in its way of bringing people the Gospel. It is legitimate. It is probably inevitable too, for Brother Charles himself never got further than drafting projects. But it is striking that what we have defined as essential remains common to all the groups, the resolute will of little brothers and little sisters to live in close contact with those who are overlooked, with "the people," as it is said today, concretely sharing the conditions of life of those whom they want to give themselves to.

This too is one of the teachings of Brother Charles's life that has an appeal wider than the circle of his direct followers. There is no doubt that he has contributed to the renewal in missionary approach that the Church is experiencing today. Long after his death he has certainly helped Christians to hear more clearly the modern world's call to them.

Perhaps it is time to give the floor back to him:

Our whole life however voiceless it may be — the life of Nazareth or the life of solitude in the desert, just as much as the public life — must preach the Gospel by example. Our whole existence, our whole being, must cry the Gospel from the rooftops. Our whole person must exude Jesus: all our acts and all our life must cry out that we belong to Jesus and be a portrait of Gospel life. All our being must be a living preaching, a reflection of Jesus, a fragrance of Jesus, something that proclaims Jesus, that shows Jesus, that shines like an image of Jesus.[21]

TWELVE

UNLESS THE GRAIN OF WHEAT DIES

On November 7, 1905, Brother Charles had written to a nun he was guiding:

I desire that the Lord might form here for the evangelization of Morocco and the Sahara and wherever else His heart may choose, a little family of brothers and one of sisters, both of which would have the same kind of life, which can be summed up in three words: imitation of Jesus' hidden life at Nazareth, perpetual adoration of the Blessed Sacrament exposed day and night, and life in the furthest corners of mission lands. I want for these brothers and sisters to be cloistered and silent, to earn their living by the work of their hands and live poorly and austerely, to make solemn vows if Rome allows it, to be very hospitable and charitable and do all the good they can without leaving their cloister. It's the way Benedictine monks and nuns evangelized Europe in the olden days that I'm dreaming of for the Moslem lands and wherever else the Heart of the Bridegroom will want them to go. I want them with a still greater poverty, a still more fervent imitation of the One and Only Beloved, with the Rule of St. Augustine rather than the Rule of St. Benedict, more silent prayer and fewer vocal ones, and last and most importantly perpetual adoration of the Blessed Sacrament.

You can guess how much I need your prayers for desires like these to come true. Pray most of all that

my wretchedness not be an obstacle to their accomplishment. It's never God who lets us down, it's
always men who let Him down. For all these desires
of mine I am alone. "The grain of wheat that dies
does not remain alone. If it dies it brings forth much
fruit."¹ Pray for me that I may die to myself so as to
bear all the fruit that Jesus wants.

We're already familiar with the projects Brother
Charles explains in this letter. But we can read here
too the way he sees his responsibility before God for
the accomplishment of these projects. "Unless the
grain of wheat dies, it remains alone." Over and over
he writes these words when he speaks of how little
visible results his life is having, and especially when he
sees that no companions are forthcoming. He has
drafted constitutions, he has written piles of letters,
putting his case to priests or religious who are wondering about their own vocations or who have the job
of guiding others. He makes notes on numerous
possibilities for evangelizing the poor around him, on
how to be present there, and on what services fraternities could offer to the Tuaregs.

It is fairly easy for us to make a certain appraisal
of all his projects, and much more intricate to
evaluate the intensity of the desires and hopes behind
them, as we're going to try to do now. Yes, in the hope
of seeing fraternities born, he thought a lot, wrote a
lot, often appealed to various people, and spent a
great deal of labor. It was not a matter of dreams and
vague wishes; to found fraternities was for Brother
Charles a task he had deeply committed his life to,
including his inner life and communion with God,
which is to say his prayer and all the effort by which
he wanted to become himself a genuine little brother
and a faithful imitator of Jesus. We know the long

hours of adoration and intercession that he spent each day in his chapel at the feet of his Beloved. Those words he repeated in his correspondence, "Pray that I may die to myself so as to bear the fruit God wants," surely tell us one of the prayers he must have presented to God with the most ardor. And the fruit he wanted to bear included his foundations. He was convinced of being responsible before Him, convinced that if those foundations didn't come to be, it was because he himself wasn't totally given or holy enough. And in the final years of his life, though he wasn't so sure any more that he was meant to accomplish those foundations, he felt at least that he had to earn them. And so he prayed, asking and begging others to pray with him and to pray for him, sure that his total conversion was what God was waiting for to bring to birth the fraternities. To Father Huvelin he wrote on June 10, 1903:

> I am still alone, dearest Father. It is because of my daily laxities, my little but numerous infidelities. And they are not little after all, for they are lacks of love and lukewarmness. It is not a little thing to be lukewarm. It is unworthy, and it is very unworthy not to love enough.

And in his touching letter to a lady in France:

> When the grain of wheat that falls does not die, it remains alone. "If it dies it bears much fruit." I have not died and so I am alone. Pray for my conversion so that by dying I may bear fruit.

> I'm here at the residence of the holy and kind Apostolic Prefect of the Sahara, and he has authorized me to work for my project in his Prefecture. In a few days I go back to my cell and the solitary tabernacle there, feeling more deeply than ever that Jesus wants me to work for the establishment of this

twofold family. Work for it how? By prayers of pleading, by self-sacrifice, by dying, by becoming holy — in short, by loving Him.

It's this that I, a sinner and unworthy to belong to the inner circle of the family, come to beg and plead that you help me with.

"Our Lord is in a hurry." His hidden life at Nazareth, so poor and lowly and prayerful, is not being imitated . . . To adore the Blessed Sacrament ought to be the cornerstone of every human being's life . . . The Sahara, eight or ten times the size of France and more populated than people think, has thirteen priests. In the interior of Morocco, the size of France with eight or ten million inhabitants, there is not a single priest nor tabernacle nor altar. "Our Lord is in a hurry." The days granted to love Him, imitate Him and save souls with Him are flying by, and people are not loving Him or imitating Him or saving with Him.[2]

Always being alone was surely a suffering for him. Not that solitude itself weighed on him; he was a man completely capable of living alone and very likely he was fairly well suited for it. It was his work he was thinking of. Sometimes he let out a soft complaint, to Mme. de Bondy, for instance. These are passages of his letters to her in 1909; modestly he no longer speaks of "fraternities" but of a companion:

How much I would like to have a companion, a priest, so that I could do better and so that this little work would go on. I don't see anyone coming.[3]

I am still alone, I have no inkling of a companion.[4]

I'm going to rebuild my hermitage in Tamanrasset to make it ready to receive a companion. He isn't showing up. I am still alone, but I keep doing all I can to have a companion.[5]

This is his suffering, rubbed raw each time

someone writes for information, gives him hope and
then disappoints. He must have expressed this sorrow
intensely in his prayer. His retreat resolutions are
another witness to the inner depths of his heart. In
1902 at Beni-Abbes he wrote:

> Do everything I can for the foundation of the maxi-
> mum number of Fraternities of the Sacred Heart of
> Jesus. To do so, become as holy as I can, do at every
> moment the most perfect thing.

> The foundation of the Little Brothers and the Little
> Sisters of the Sacred Heart depends on me, on my
> faithfulness and my conversion . . . Lord, convert me!
> Blessed Virgin, Saint Joseph, Saint Magdelene, I put
> my soul in your hands. What I can do to glorify God
> the most and to save souls for His sake, is to found
> the Little Brothers and the Little Sisters of the Sacred
> Heart. And to do so one thing is necessary and
> sufficient: to become holy.

"Do everything I can," "become holy for it,"
"pray and suffer in order to establish, to promote, to
sanctify . . . " These phrases come back year after year
in his retreat resolutions until 1909, the last ones that
have come down to us, signs of how unwaveringly he
recognized in himself a founder's mission, or at least
a mission to prepare the foundation and earn its
coming. "Because the hidden life of Jesus is not
imitated," "because thousands of souls need to be
saved" — these are the motives he speaks of. He
wants fraternities, or rather he thinks God wants
these fraternities, and he strives to put his heart and
his whole life in unison with this desire of God's. He
prays earnestly, he offers his life, he sacrifices himself.

In his letter we read these words, "I have not died
and so I am alone . . . Pray that by dying I may bear
fruit." It was dying to himself by total self-denial that

he was talking about. But after a life so relentlessly austere and dispossessed, through such accessibility and solitude and faithfulness, was he not already indeed dead to himself when the hour came that evening of December 1, 1916, for him to pour out his blood literally in the sand of the Sahara, his land of adoption? As early as June 6, 1897, he had written in his meditations:

> Think that you are to die a martyr, stripped of everything, stretched out on the ground, naked and unrecognizable, covered with wounds and blood, cruelly and violently slain, and desire that it be today.

In a letter he wrote on the very morning of his death we can read again that same thought, which had become familiar to him:

> When we are reduced to nothing it is the most powerful means we have to unite ourselves with Jesus and to do good to souls.[6]

Today several congregations of little brothers and little sisters have sprung up in the Church. There are fraternities throughout the world, and secular institutes and numerous other groups besides, which claim Charles de Foucauld as their founder. They all desire to travel a road he opened up; they all recognize an example in him; they all know that through his life they have discovered a way for them today to live the Gospel. All sense too that there is a secret correlation between certain shining lights that the Spirit is giving to the Church of our times and the intercession, the sacrifices and the immolation of Brother Charles.

> If the grain of wheat dies,
> it brings forth much fruit.

PART III

THE FRATERNITIES IN THE WORLD

THE FRATERNITIES
THROUGHOUT THE WORLD

Brother Charles died in 1916 without any followers. In 1933 in Montpellier, France, the Little Sisters of the Sacred Heart took up the Rule of 1902 and began to base their religious life on it. Today they have fraternities in North and Central Africa, in Latin America, and in European countries as well.

That same year, 1933, René Voillaume and 4 companions left France for the Sahara and that group became the core of the Little Brothers of Jesus. In 1939, Little Sister Magdeleine, in a different part of the Sahara, started the Little Sisters of Jesus. From those beginnings the Little Brothers of the Gospel and the Little Sisters of the Gospel were also to evolve. It is the story of these latter 4 Fraternities that we will tell in the following pages, in the words first of Brother Rene and Little Sister Magdeleine, and then of other Brothers and Sisters, out of their daily lives.

Interview with René Voillaume

How did you come to know of Brother Charles?

"Charles de Foucauld was first known because of the dramatic way he died — it was in all the big newspapers — and then mainly through the book by Rene Bazin which came out in 1921. Today it's hard to imagine the effect that book had on youth then. It reached a whole generation of French youth. It set a whole spiritual movement going.

"I was 16 then and studying philosophy in Versailles. I can remember well (when something has turned your life upside down you always remember well) the place in my room where I used to keep the book about Charles de Foucauld. The book had moved me that much.

"Besides, it was during a time when I was searching for my vocation. A question had been working on me since before 1921. I felt attracted by Benedictine life, then I changed and was attracted by the Blessed Sacrament Fathers, by the Eucharist. I couldn't find anything that completely satisfied me. That was where the biography of Brother Charles came in and made everything take shape. I knew right away that that was it.

"I didn't dare bring it up to my director, but I finally did write him a letter during summer vacation. He answered me that I should have told him about it sooner! But think what it's like to be a 17 year old boy. Nobody was going to let me set off and follow Brother Charles just like that."

In fact René Voillaume entered the diocesan seminary of Paris; he kept his secret for a while. Two years later he entered the White Fathers (as the congregation of the Fathers of Africa were then called) to do his novitiate, but with the firm intention of "afterwards following a vocation on the inspiration of Brother Charles." The White Fathers accepted him. Because of a sickness René Voillaume came back to Paris to finish theology studies. The long period of preparation continued. Other seminarians got the same idea. A group formed. They tried to put together constitutions and a rule. One day a White Father gave them a precious black notebook in which Brother Charles had written, in 1899, the Constitutions of the Little Brothers of the Sacred Heart and the article by article commentary on it.

"That was a moving moment for us. It made a deep impression on us to see the handwriting of Charles de Foucauld for the first time, to have his notebook in our hands, to have a rule so rooted in the Gospel. We were completely won over and it no longer occurred to us that we could look in a different direction."

When the group consulted the superior of the seminary, they were disappointed. He said, "This rule was written for angels, not for human beings." They went on planning and then made direct preparations: studying Arabic at Rome and Tunis, contacting people who had known Brother Charles, then choosing a place to settle in Algeria. The White Fathers guided them toward the Ksour region of Algeria, north of the Sahara itself. The choice fell on El-Abiodh Sidi Cheikh.

What of the foundations then?

"After the ceremony when the first five of us took the habit at Montmartre, the shrine dedicated to the Sacred Heart in the middle of Paris, we reached El-Abiodh Sidi Cheikh right at the beginning of October 1933. I had been elected Prior and was in charge of the foundation. We moved into a bordj which had formerly served as a little fort. There were 8 rooms arranged, as I remember, in a horseshoe around a little yard with a wall on the fourth side. We placed the Blessed Sacrament in one of the rooms and the first Mass was celebrated on the feast of St. Bruno,

October 6. We settled down there and began to observe our rule. The rule consisted of perpetual silence and cloister, except for a once-a-week walk and going to visit the sick. The timetable was: Prime on rising, Terce at the end of the morning followed by Mass, None about 3 p.m., Vespers in the evening, Compline before going to bed. We got up at 1 a.m., said Matins, exposed the Blessed Sacrament and had an hour of adoration, said Lauds, and went back to bed at 2:30 or 20 till 3. During the day there was adoration, work, gardening, and we had also started a dispensary.

"What we were living there was a cloistered life along the lines of the Rule of 1899, but broadly supplemented by a spirituality and customs that we had received through our contacts with the Carthusians.

"Right away we tackled the problem of adaptation, for that was one of our concerns. For what to wear there was no problem; we took the garb of the country — turban and the flowing gown called a burnous. We started to learn prayers in Arabic. Everybody set to studying Arabic and we also used a certain number of Arabic songs. But back then the liturgy could not be varied much and we still had to use Latin for the office.

"We were also influenced by Carmelite spirituality even from the first year. Thus we aimed for a balance between life in common and periods of hermitage according to the customs and traditions of Carmelite life and its "times of desert."

"We went out to stay in the desert, not to a fixed site with a hermitage house, but under a tent the way nomads do. I made the first try, and I set out with a guide, a tent, and two camels, and I spent a week in the desert. Later on each of us regularly made retreats like that, often for prolonged periods. We would take turns staying 3 weeks in the desert, at least as far away as four days' walk.

"The War came. Some of us were drafted and we found ourselves separated. That along with the events happening all around us, led us to ask ourselves if we were really living what Brother Charles had wanted since in fact he had never lived the way we were. We weren't living from the work of our hands, we weren't forming little groups by the ideal Brother Charles had so often expressed when he said he wanted the brothers to imitate Jesus' family at Nazareth. As you see, it wasn't right away that we really grasped all of Brother Charles' intuitions.

"I should add that the different steps of our evolution were also inspired by the context of the Church. Up to the date of the foundation at El-Abiodh in 1933, we had been deeply marked by the missionary thrust Pius XI had given to the Church and by the desire he had expressed too that contemplative vocations find a place in the missions. There was also a great current fostering adaptation. Those were the days of Father Lebbe and his work in China and Pius XI had just consecrated the first Chinese bishops.

"Around the time when we were starting in El-Abiodh there were in Europe the great movements of the Young Christian Workers and the Catholic Action. A little later during the War the Mission de France and the Mission de Paris were founded for the evangelization of working people, and soon there would be the first worker-priests. If all that had not been going on, would we Little Brothers have taken the step we did?

"Besides there was my encounter with Little Sister Magdeleine and the Little Sisters of Jesus. It all came together into a first foundation at Aix-en-Provence that was a real innovation. We replaced the monastic habit by lay clothes and we got jobs as workers. At the same time the Little Sisters were starting to work in factories at Marseilles and at Aix. From then on the foundations have multiplied along the lines of little contemplative fraternities in the midst of the poor in all the countries of the world."

Why the Little Brothers and the Little Sisters of the Gospel?

"That's a hard question to answer in a way that satisfies everybody because both the Little Brothers of Jesus and the Fraternities of the Gospel are evolving now. I'll just describe the circumstances that gave rise to the Little Brothers and the Little Sisters of the Gospel.

"Briefly, there were vocations coming to us who were attracted by our ideal of religious life, conceiving it as a presence in small groups that share the way of life of the poor, but who wanted to combine it with their desire for evangelizing work. Besides that, the experience of some fraternities of Little Brothers of Jesus had put us in front of a kind of urgent need for evangelization. By the mere fact that Little Brothers or Little Sisters of Jesus had been living among certain peoples for a number of years, they themselves had begun to be ready for evangelization. This was especially true in foundations in the midst of isolated peoples whom the Gospel had never reached — a tribe in Mora in the North Cameroons,, Pygmies in what is today Zaire, then the Makiritare Indians of Venezuela.

"When we felt this need, we had a clear notion that the Little Brothers of Jesus were not to undertake an organized ministry, and yet that evangelization required some sort of ministry. That was what the Little Brothers of the Gospel were first called, by the way, Little Brothers of Ministry. Then we added, Little Brothers of the Ministry of the Gospel, and finally came up with Little Brothers of the Gospel.

"To say more would require on one hand a whole history of the evolution of the conditions in which Little Brothers of Jesus have been living in their various fraternities, and on the other hand the evolution of the Little Brothers of the Gospel whose concept of evangelization has changed as the problems the Church is meeting in accomplishing her mission changes."

It was in June 1956 that the first fraternity of Little Brothers of the Gospel was founded, in Sambric, a little village in southern Europe. The first fraternity of the Little Sisters of the Gospel was founded in 1963 in Venezuela.

Little Sister Magdeleine tells her story:

The whole story of the foundation can be summed up in these few words: "God took me by the hand and blindly I followed . . . " It was in what seemed the most total darkness and the most disconcerting absence of human means, but in a limitless confidence in the Power of Jesus, Master of the Impossible.

God had prepared me since I was a young child, calling me first to Him, then teaching me a love for Africa and at the same time a love for the least, the poorest, the most forsaken of peoples.

I read René Bazin's book on Brother Charles as soon as it came out, since I was in touch with the White Fathers and White Sisters of El Golea, which in those days was the farthest outpost.

But obstacles piled up against any plans for my future: 4 years when World War I decimated a large part of my family, 10 years when I was sick and bedridden, 6 more years because of my mother whom I couldn't leave alone. It wasn't till after 20 years of waiting that God's chosen time came at last.

Twenty years of waiting! Only someone who has really been through it can realize what those words contain of trust alternating with anguish.

The only light shining in that dark period was the story of Brother Charles's life and his writings in which I had found the whole ideal I was dreaming of for my life: the Gospel as a way of life, total poverty, a hidden life in the midst of forsaken peoples. And above all, love in all its fullness: Jesus Caritas, Jesus Love. I begged the Lord to let me set out quickly for the land of Islam, for the Sahara or the Hoggar, to look for the footsteps of Little Brother Charles of Jesus and to live a life like his there. I was sure the Lord was calling me to become one of those Little Sisters that Brother Charles had desired so much and whose founder he clearly was to be "by suppliant prayer, by self-sacrifice, by dying, in short, by loving."

After 20 years of waiting God's time came at last.

On October 6, 1936, in an overflowing joy, I arrived at Marseilles to set sail for Algiers, taking with me not only my first companion, Sister Anne, but also my elderly mother, for I was her sole support and I couldn't leave her behind alone.

As soon as we got to Algiers we providentially met a priest. He was pastor in Boghari and thus we

found our way to this little town 100 miles from
Algiers where we settled very poorly. The priest's
desire was that we set up a service center: workshop
for learning a trade, dispensary, soup line. It quickly
grew to extended proportions.

We decided to dedicate several days a week to
visiting in a 12 mile radius around Boghari sometimes
under the tents in the scrub-grass desert and sometimes in the dugout huts in the mountains where no
European had ever penetrated. These were the only
days that really corresponded for me to the vocation I
had glimpsed and come looking for.

It was during these long tours, on foot the first
year, on horseback the second, that my projects took
shape. In my mind it wasn't at all going to be a new
Congregation but simply a very small group among
whom I could realize my personal vocation.

For two years we defied our bodies and lived in a
whirlwind of activity. But we quickly saw that in such
an activity something essential was missing for us: the
time to be quiet and pray.

Yet the Lord had given me a vocation to be a
contemplative in the midst of the life of the Muslim
world to make the Lord present there as our Lady did
at the Visitation. It was the vocation of Little Brother
Charles of Jesus, who even when he was intensely
active, remained one of the greatest contemplatives
of his age.

In March 1938 we thought of participating in the
pilgrimage to El-Goléa for the blessing on the 19th of
March of the new Church of St. Joseph built at the
site of Brother Charles' tomb.

It grew into a project of a pilgrimage of prayer
and penance to beg the Lord to help us to know His
Will and to accomplish it.

At El Goléa we first met Father Voillaume, the founder and Prior General of the Little Brothers of the Sacred Heart (that is how the Congregation of the Little Brothers of Jesus was first called), who had come from El Abiodh by camel. Bishop Nouet, the Apostolic Prefect from Ghardaia whom I had been writing to for 10 years about the Sahara my life's dream, was also at the ceremony. To both of them I spoke about my vocation to be a follower of Little Brother Charles telling them that the service center in Boghari didn't completely correspond to it.

And next thing, when we got back to Boghari we learned that a Congregation of Sisters was ready to come and take over everything the two of us had gotten started.

It was a sign of God. But it made us realize that our hearts were more attached than we thought to that place in Boghari, to all the friends young and grown-up, sick and elderly, whom we were going to leave.

We decided to go to Algiers and see Bishop Nouet, and I reminded him of his promise to take us in his jurisdiction in the Sahara if Boghari were closed to us.

I explained to him that meanwhile I had been haunted by the idea of going away for a few months to a religious Novitiate house to have a time of silence and prayer to refresh my spiritual strength after the overactivity of Boghari, and above all to prepare myself to lead a consecrated life. I had no idea though of founding a new congregation, such an idea had never entered my head.

Bishop Nouet asked admission for the two of us for six months in the Novitiate of the White Sisters, near Algiers. Then a few months later he decided that we would do the complete year of canonical novitiate, advising us to make profession, for he preferred to receive us in the Sahara as sisters, rather than lay-women. And he asked me to write Constitutions.

That was the birth of the Little Sisters of Jesus, decreed thus by the only voice that had the authority to represent for me the Will of God, without any personal intentions of mine mixed in with it. And that matched the vocation I had always had but which health and family reasons had prevented me from following.

But I thought it was going to mean just founding a fraternity of nomad Little Sisters in the Sahara, who would be poor, very poor, living part of the year under the tent.

I made profession with Sister Anne on September 8, 1939, in the White Sisters' house just after the war between France and Germany was declared. That day of September 8, 1939, is considered as the date of the foundation of the Little Sisters of Jesus.

Bishop Nouet offered us a choice between Ghardaia, Ouargla and Touggourt. He left us free but he strongly emphasized his preference for Touggourt. We had only to let ourselves be led. It was there in a place called Sidi Boujnan, in the middle of the desert among the tents, and right beside a little spring-water well that was a meeting place for all the nomads of the region that the Lord had chosen a place for us, ratifying, better than we ever could have, our name of nomad Little Sisters which will always be what people call us.

A few months later Bishop Nouet spoke to me about the need for a novitiate house somewhere outside the Sahara.

In December 1940 the first five novices gathered at Lyon-Ste-Foy where a religious congregation took us in. In September 1941 our own Novitiate was set up in Aix-en-Provence.

In July 1946 I became certain that the Fraternity had to spread out to the whole world and become "universal," all the while keeping its original consecration to the Muslims to whom a fourth of the fraternities and a fourth of the Little Sisters must be dedicated.

From that time on the Fraternity grew very quickly and less than 10 years later it had spread to all 6 continents. Today there are 1300 Little Sisters in more than 200 fraternities.

A Letter from Brother René Page (successor to Brother René Voillaume as Prior of the Little Brothers of Jesus)

Jesus' life at Nazareth has been our inspiration for a religious life which is exclusively dedicated to God, but also one in which we are poor among the poor. What does that mean? The challenge which the Gospel puts before us and which we should wholeheartedly accept, is that of a religious life without compromise lived in the context of the common life of ordinary men and women.

I speak deliberately of a challenge, for God's attitude towards us goes against a certain worldly way of looking at things and people, which we all too easily share without fully realizing it. For example, don't we at times ask ourselves if it's really possible after all to reconcile two things as apparently different as religious life and life among the people, not to mention the added difficulty of a contemplative life in such conditions? If so, it could be a sign that we haven't yet learned to know God as He really is and that we don't believe enough in his love. The people God loves are precisely those people we meet daily in the streets and on the job. God calls each one to Himself, all of them just as they are, with their qualities and faults, their joys and sorrows. He calls them all to share His own inner life, to be perfect as He Himself is perfect. There's no second-class call to something less, but only the one vocation to the infinite joy of God's very self, for God's love has no restrictions. One of the essential points of a genuinely contemplative life is this knowledge of God and of His love, and the realization that He is little concerned with human greatness. Lord and Master of the universe that He is, when He came among us to reveal to us His heart's secrets and to give His life for us, he was not ashamed to appear as a humble and ordinary man. God-among-us was a man of the people. We have no need of being ashamed before Him of our poor humanity or our humble condition of life. He didn't find in them any obstacle to the full expression of His life. That in fact is the basis of evangelical poverty. It's something noble and great, quite the opposite from some sort of humiliating resignation. It's a source of joy and hope founded on the certitude of being loved by Someone who knows us well, respects us, and desires our highest good far more than we do ourselves. It's a joy and hope offered to all, for the renewal of each and the renewal of the face of the earth.

Why am I insisting on all this? Because if we are to accept without reserve our conditions of life, we must first realize what kind of a love God has for us. If we want to share authentically, as brothers, the life of the poorest and most neglected, we must first of all surrender our own littleness and worthlessness to God's love and put all our hope in Him alone.

In choosing this simple attitude before Jesus, an attitude within anyone's reach, we become saviors with Him. Jesus' work reached its crowning point on the Cross of Calvary, and our salvation was achieved at that hour when "all was consummated." But Jesus is savior from the moment of His birth among us. The cross didn't fall into Jesus' life like something foreign or unexpected. It was no accident. Jesus was born poor, born into a poor family and in the poverty of the stable. His family wasn't even under their own roof when He was born. Afterwards, He spent the whole of his life within this situation of poverty. Already in His simple condition as a worker, Jesus had taken up His cross. Not the shame-filled cross of Good Friday, but the cross Jesus was talking about when He said in the Gospel, "If anyone wants to come after me, let him take up his cross daily and follow me." The cross Jesus took at Nazareth already put its mark on his birth at Bethlehem. It is the ordinary cross all men must bear, whatever their condition: grief, toil, sweat, all those useless sorrows, all those sufferings the world is full of and which are as varied as men are. These are all the crosses that don't make any show, that others often don't know about, but which are ours in their mystery. It's this ordinary cross that Jesus made His in His life at Nazareth. It's by means of this cross that He was already accomplishing the redemption His Father had put into His hands. Afterwards during His public life His work of salvation by the cross was precipitated, you might say, and He carried it to the extreme in rejection, humiliation, persecution, and finally death on Calvary. When they crucified Him they wrote on the cross, "Jesus of Nazareth."

When you look at Jesus' life like this and see "Jesus of Nazareth" in the unity of the work by which He saved us, you'll understand that imitating Jesus at Nazareth is something very concrete. You'll see that it can take up our whole life, and everything in our life, making us "saviors with Jesus."

Little Brothers of Jesus on a fishing trawler:

Dear Brothers,

I have been wanting to spend a few minutes with you for some time now. And I am doing so today, conscious of the fact that it will not take my mind away from Jesus, since thinking of all of you is part of the same movement.

I have just made the Way of the Cross, curled up on my bunk with my face to the partition, leaning against my pillow. There are a small and unobtrusive icon and a crucifix to help me to fix my attention. Last night between two spells on watch or working in the hold, I was able to read the breviary, and this morning again I succeeded in saying and meditating on the liturgical prayers in spite of the music coming out of my nearest bunk-mate's transistor radio.

But obviously, the best time for recollection is when everybody is asleep. And in a crew's room which serves as dormitory, recreation room, sitting room and refectory all together and where there are continual comings and goings with the changes of watch or work shifts, it is very, very difficult to take any more time away from one's already scanty hours of sleep. At the same time, I have noticed that when the great liturgical feasts come along there is a special gust from the Holy Spirit to sustain us in our prayer against the unwelcome light, the noise of the transistor radios and the noise of the engine, the shaking of the hull, the rolling of the boat or the card game going on at the nearest table.

It is 2 o'clock in the morning and I have only done half of my night shift. We are on our return voyage. Our present expedition is nearing its end. We came out on July 13, and will be at the next port on the 26th, probably late in the afternoon. The haul so far amounts to nothing, 12 tons of fish.

You get to know the smallest details of your boat. We of the crew got to know each other, too. The crew has scarcely changed in the past three years, and we live together continually, day and night. As often happens in such close quarters, each one's little problems and the differences between characters take on exaggerated proportions, especially towards the end of an expedition when everybody's nerves are more or less on edge from fatigue and lack of sleep; and still more so, of course when the haul has been meager like this time and the sea has been bad.

Our work days are very irregular as to hours, but are never less than 12 hours and sometimes 18 or 20. When nearing the end of an expedition you feel it in your muscles because it takes more than the windlass and tackle to bring everything on board — it takes a lot of effort.

Periods of intensive work are not too conducive to prayer, of course. You have to recuperate first and you don't feel so much like composing poems about the immensity of the sea, the changing colors of the water or the sound of the winds in the masts. What I miss most is silence and solitude. I'll welcome my leave and the chance to be with a brother in a quiet fraternity for a while.

I wish I could talk to you about my friends. I mean each member of the crew from the chief down to the ship's boy. Everyone lives very much by himself and for himself. There is of course a certain amount of sharing of worries, as of work, but friendship goes far beyond that: it is a real sharing and doubtless has to be earned gradually. What remains then, if not the fact of knowing that you have given yourself to God and continue to feel the desire to belong to him and to reach him, the desire to beg him constantly to fill in the deficiencies and restore calm and joy in an existence almost as changeable as the sea.

Your brother on the seas,
Michel

From Moncton, New Brunswick,
The Little Sisters of Jesus:

It was in July, 1973, that Jesus led us to Moncton, a small-sized city on the Atlantic coasts of Canada. Our neighborhood is made of a dozen barracks in rows, formerly an army camp. It is a neighborhood of transients where everybody is waiting to find something better.

Life is hard and lonely here. Most of our neighbors are young women, left to bear the heavy responsibility of a family alone. There are a few elderly people with only their unhappy memories for companionship, some teenagers getting tougher as they grow up, and the little ones, who come to us full of trust, asking for nothing more than to be listened to or rocked in our arms for a little while. Often their faces make us ashamed of our adult world which has wounded them, and they cry out to us that our society of abundance exists only so that some may live in luxury.

We are two little sisters here. While one is staying at home to keep house and be available to the neighbors around, the other one is working to earn our living in a big warehouse which specializes in wholesale food and cleaning products. It's a job which plunges us into the midst of a deep sickness of our society. We certainly aren't proud to realize that they sell more cigarettes and vitamin-enriched cat and dog food than staple foods. In contrast to that there are the faces of our neighbors, and of our starving brothers and sisters all over the world.

Daily life has brought us into deep friendship with our neighbors, without our needing to talk much. Ann and Peter: she is 20 years old and he's 26. Both of them had a miserable childhood, deeply marked by the contempt that everyone had for the neighborhood where they lived. They drink a lot to forget or to try to face a world which has no place for the weak, and tells them so. Kay and Joe: she's 16, he's 20. When he was 12 years old, Joe disappeared onto the streets of Montreal and Toronto; their miseries met, and soon a child will be born. Cyndy, 19 years old, is coming to trust us more and more. Her face and her heart already bear the imprints of violence and life in prison, but it's so wonderful too to see how respect and gentleness can make her eyes light up. Mary has moved away with her three children to a village on the coast. We're touched to see how faithfully she comes back to visit us, for it's like a call never to betray our respect for those who are used to being looked down on. She's only 22.

We learn from all of them, day after day: the amazing way that those who have so little help out those who have nothing, their marvelous ability to find a little bit of happiness in the simplest things, the way they welcome everyone without judging, their courage to go on living in spite of so many unsolved problems. Within us we feel deeply the desire that one day we will be worthy to say "we" when we speak of "them."

Our lives are made up of lots of friendship, lots of silence, lots of listening, and many things which we can bring to Jesus during our time of adoration each day. Our adoration is mingled with the noise of life going on in the neighborhood, and the times of prayer have to find their place in the schedule of a poor working person, along with time to drop in and visit friends and neighbors. We try to be present to God and to people around us, peacefully and without counting the cost.

A little sister's life is very simple and very ordinary. It is because of Jesus that we are here, and so even the most commonplace things are linked with God, and can speak of him. Since Jesus willed to live the life of Nazareth, that gives meaning to our own life, which could otherwise appear useless. It is Brother Charles's heritage:

> "In order to be a leaven of hope, bury yourselves away silently. Seek no efficacity but that of giving a little more joy and love to those around you. When someone meets you, may he discover that God loves him and that he is unique in the world . . . "

Little Sister Magdeleine, the Foundress of
The Little Sisters of Jesus, writes to them:

Little Sisters:

Do you understand what it means for a religious to have been called to live poor among the poor, leading an everyday life in the midst of mankind, and to live it as "leaven in the dough"?[1]

Until now it seemed as if religious life could not be lived in this way, but I say to you:

You have only one Model: Jesus. Do not look for another.

Like Jesus during his life on earth, make yourself "all things to all men." An Arab in the midst of Arabs, a nomad among nomads, a worker among working people, but above all be human among your fellow men. Do not think that living among people will hinder your life of union with God.

Penetrate deeply among people by sharing their life, by friendship and by love. Give yourself completely to them, like Jesus who came to serve and not to be served. You too, become one with them. Then you will be like leaven which must love itself in the dough to make it rise.

The way that Little Brother Charles leads us is not new, unless we think that to follow Jesus as he did is something new. He chose one Model: Jesus. He had one Leader, one Master only: Jesus. He will tell you only one thing is necessary: to love Jesus.

He will tell you to "walk with your feet in his footprints," "your hand in his hand" "to live his life" "lovingly to reproduce his likeness." He will ask you that by the grace of God you let yourself be so penetrated by Jesus' spirit that "you think his thoughts, speak his words, do as he did; in short that you disappear so that through you he may speak and act with his own Heart and Will.

When he speaks to you of obedience, he will ask you to become one with Jesus, as Jesus was one with the Father. When he speaks of poverty and humility, he will speak of the poverty and humility of Jesus, who made himself the least of all and the servant of all. When he speaks of chastity, he will ask you to give yourself completely to your beloved Brother and Lord Jesus. Then your capacities for loving, freed from all ties, will find total fulfillment in Divine Love. Your vows are not to separate you from your brothers and Christ's but to consecrate you more completely to all the members of his mystical body.

Your fraternity will have to be a home bright with love like the first fraternity where Jesus lived at Nazareth. It will have to be a home where He is the center, the intimate Friend, the Brother, and at the same time the sovereign Master and beloved Lord. You will pray at His feet; you will work along side Him; you will rest in His company.

Your charity will be the result of your life of deep fellowship with Jesus, the source of all love. Your apostolate will be to bear witness to Jesus, letting your life express His love and His presence in the Blessed Sacrament and the Gospel.

And Jesus will become the one passion of your life, as he became the one passion of the life of Little Brother Charles of Jesus. This boundless love summed up in ;his motto, "Jesus-Caritas — Jesus-Love," will identify you with Christ Jesus to the point of becoming one with Him. He in you and you in Him, you will be able to say with St. Paul the Apostle, "It is no longer I who live but it is Christ who lives in me."[2]

From the Little Brothers of the Gospel
In Frankfort, Germany:

Hermann:
Our rhythm of life has changed a lot since we moved in three years ago. We have more and more

friends and visitors. Sometimes when I come back from work, I can't seem to muster enough courage to start something else. But why should it be different for me than for my co-workers who are also tired and worn down by the heavy, monotonous work?

A year and a half at the paint factory has helped me get to know what it means to be a worker and understand workers better. Sharing someone's life is the only way you can really understand.

This time in my letter I want to tell you what it's like in the shop and what I've experienced. Let me say right away that the atmosphere in the shop is a bad one and we all suffer from it. Part of it comes from the working conditions. But the main cause is the difference of situation between the German-born workers and the immigrants. The nationals almost always have higher jobs and more privileges. The bosses treat them much better too. The immigrants, who have to do the heavy work, are not taken seriously. Prejudices, differences in mentalities, and difficulties of understanding also come into it. Lately there've also been worries about keeping our jobs (with the fall in the market, production in my department has really slowed down). Immigrants used to be called "Gastarbeider," — guest workers — but now nobody wants "guests." In all conflicts that break out I try when I can to bring a little reconciliation. I feel it like the Lord's call because I work mainly with immigrants but at the same time am in a position to reach the nationals since I speak German. And being Austrian I'm not considered a 100% immigrant. But to avoid any ambiguity about justice, I quickly saw that I was obliged to place myself clearly on the side of the immigrants and they soon counted me a friend.

Jean-Francois:

I still work at the same factory. It will soon be

three years that I've been working in the same department, shipping the dyes, where I always do the same thing, packing my samples. It's monotonous work, often alone, but fortunately there are the coffee breaks and the other chances to be together with my co-workers.

At noon in the canteen I often eat with the Italian guys. My Italian is getting better but I haven't caught on yet to the dialects.

The atmosphere in the shop is not too bad but one thing is clear: the immigrants don't have any of the responsibilities, and the bosses make them sweat.

Still and all, I'm getting much closer too to my German-born co-workers than at the beginning. Sometimes we might go and have a beer together after work. That never could have happened two years ago.

Hermann:

We're glad when our friendships from the factory are carried over into the rest of our life. It's mostly the immigrant guys who stop in to visit at the fraternity or invite us to their places. Many had to leave their families back in their country. They live alone and suffer from their solitude. The German-born workers have families for the most part and a number of friends. Often they live fairly far from the factory out in new developments where they have a house and their own yard.

Our neighborhood is mostly peopled by immigrants and old folks. There are still a few German families who didn't want to leave their old house, but most have moved out to the suburbs. It's a neighborhood you get to love, like a village within the city, little houses all the same, narrow streets cars can hardly get through, to the delight of the children who can play there undisturbed. You hardly ever see that in today's Germany. In fact the neighborhood doesn't have a very good reputation, mainly because so many foreigners live there and also because the housing is old and cramped. All the nationalities of immigrants in Germany are represented here: Yugoslavs, Greeks, Italians, Spaniards, Moroccans. We have lots of friends among them. Back-breaking work, far from wife or kids and in the midst of it all they keep a cheerfulness, a quality of hospitality, and a simplicity that amazes us time and again.

Jean-Francois:

With so many friends our life can get pretty busy and often we have to juggle things to keep for ourselves some moments for a time of adoration. We often have to play it by ear and know how to grab the free intervals. And our "praying without ceasing," has to be intense, that is, a contemplative way of seeing events and people. But it's not possible without time-outs for prayer and this is one of the reasons our days "in the desert" help me a lot.

Sometimes it's also hard to find time to be together just among Brothers and talk about things. Here too we grab our chances. Little by little the friendship among us is growing deeper. Yet there's always the danger, not of clashes between us (that's nothing serious because we work them out) but of superficiality in our relationships or not trusting one another enough. If I'm not open with my brothers the way I am with certain of my friends, there's something wrong.

Hermann:

There are three of us now since last October. Berthold, who is German, came after his novitiate and that's had a very positive effect on our life. But we're having to make an effort so that our life together will deepen. That requires pursuing our exchanges. It's not enough to say the Office together. In our rhythm of life, the desert day takes on a lot of importance. We don't have a hermitage, but we can get away to a retreat house nearby.

Most of my co-workers know now that I'm a religious brother, or that I'm somehow connected with the Church. But the word "a religious" seems completely foreign to them. You can't shut your eyes to how far away the Church is from them. None of them are asking themselves what a living Christian faith is because it's something they've hardly ever encountered around them. And they have other interests in the front of their minds. Then, those among the immigrants who come from traditionally Catholic countries like Italy and Spain aren't at home in this broadly secularized surrounding, and they drop all religious practice. For the guys at work it's something altogether new, religious that work like them.

To evangelize means before all else for me to give witness to our life with God and to our hope, to enter into the mystery of Christ's incarnation in order to be close to my co-workers. That means a constant conversion too, and letting their expectations stimulate me because they're not merely "unbelievers" whom it's up to us to "convert." You find in them too Christian values like simplicity, uprightness, availability, and sharing. My friendship has to be so respectful that it reveals to them the seeds of the Gospel that they are already living.

Letter from The Little Sisters of Jesus in Niger,
A Tent Fraternity with the Toubou Nomads:

Little Brother Charles had desired that there be
"semi-nomad" Sisters, and when Little Sister Magdeleine founded the Fraternity she had first intended it
exclusively for the nomads of the Sahara.

The first tent fraternity started in March 1950 at
El Abiodh, south of Oran on the edge of the Great
Western Sand Desert among the Arab nomads of the
tribe of the Ouled Sidi Cheikh, whose tents are made
of bands woven of sheep wool and sewn together.

Other tent fraternities followed:

In the Hoggar, in the very region where Little
Brother Charles lived among the Tuaregs where the
tents are made of skins, dyed red and tanned.

In Niger in the region of Kerboubou not far from
Agadez among the Southern Tuareg tribes where the
tents are made of straw mats.

There have been other tent fraternities in Somali-
land and Jordan, but the political situation of the
countries didn't allow us to go on with our nomad life.

What allowed each one of these fraternities to
become quickly a real part of things is the sharing of
the life of our friends under the same conditions. Like
them we live under the tent and we have a flock of
sheep or goats, which is more or less arduous to
shepherd depending on the region, the season, the
grazing conditions.

Like them we have to go sometimes far to get
water and wood with our donkeys. Like all nomad
women we have to keep up the tents, which means
weaving or tanning or braiding, depending on the
country. And there is the various everyday work:
cooking (couscous of wheat or millet porridge),

making butter, cheese and bread, which takes a lot of time. We weave the wool too as well as the goats hair and the camels hair which we use to make the indispensible ropes for tying up the tents and pickets when we travel.

Now we're writing you about the joy of a new tent fraternity. Our fraternity with the Toubous is underway.

After four months at N'guigmi making our tent, studying the language and getting to know the camping places around, we were ready to go. Moussa, who is 16 or 17, was a big help to us.

The day came and we got everything ready in the courtyard of our little house at N'Guigmi. It was afternoon when Moussa came with a big smile, "The camels are there." We were excited, but not frantic, for everything was ready and some boys helped us load it all. In the street in front of our house people gathered in surprise.

"You're going out to the bush in this cold?"

"Yes, why not? Aren't there people in the bush now? The cold is the same for them, they're people like you and me."

"What you say is true. Wuce, wuce." (We encourage you).

Except for a moment's emotion when a young camel was startled by the noise of an automobile and frightened the others, everything went well. Each man took his place on the back of the camels and the caravan got underway. A little boy was on the first camel, and we followed on foot. The two little sisters who would be staying at N'Guigmi came along with us part of the way. It's such a great joy for this nomad fraternity to be starting.

No problems on the way. Moussa rode on the

second loaded camel to keep in balance the trunk that was always leaning "to the west," as he said.

Less than two hours walk and we could catch a glimpse of the camp. All three of us felt our hearts beating as we arrived. So many unknown things before us. Trusting confidence in the Lord and in our brothers the Toubous. And such a love in our hearts.

At last we were there. Moussa led the caravan to the tree we had chosen last Sunday for our tent. We held the loads steady while the camels knelt and the children jumped off nimbly. The sun had set. Night was close. A cold, strong wind was coming up. And suddenly from all the tents the women came toward us. Moussa's father was there too. We greeted one another while we all unloaded the baggage. Two women were already sweeping under the tree. Other women took a picket each and in a quarter of an hour we had made a shelter for the night with a big mat. They arranged our baggage around the shelter and inside. We worked along with them in wonder. It was truly an extraordinary experience we won't be able to forget.

"Whoever welcomes you, welcomes Me." (Matt. 10:40) Lord, the Toubous have welcomed you, and with what heart.

After a moment from the tent compound of Maydouyey and Armata (Moussa's mother) they brought us millet cakes, two dishes of hot food, milk and water. Two women, one of whom was very old, had already brought us wood.

Our prayer that evening was full of thanksgiving. We can no longer put up with hearing "the Toubous are this, the Toubous are that." No, because the Toubous, that means Moussa, Armata, Ibrahim. There aren't any Toubous in general.

This beginning is a source of grace for each of us little sisters. Arriving there humanly so powerless is the occasion to renew our sense of what our vocation means and why we've chosen this life. These people were living here serenely; they weren't expecting anything from us. What have we come to do? To live in their midst a sort of season of Advent, in their name. Through our consecrated lives, to consecrate ordinary Toubou life. To give our life to Jesus in the simplest, most everyday way, so that he may be "Toubou in the midst of Toubous."

A little corner of our tent serves as the chapel. Behind the curtain you can see a skin laid on a mat. Immediately people know that it means prayer. A neighbor lady told us her surprise the first days, "So then Europeans too speak of God." And we had a long talk, speaking in Haussa, the lingua franca, telling her that our life is all because of God. I realize that we're lucky that our life is such that Jesus is the only way to explain it.

It may seem astonishing when you think of the drought they suffer from so terribly, but our neighbors didn't ask us for any kind of material aid, medicines or food or whatever. Moussa kept telling us the first days, "No, don't make tea for my sister, you'll have to put all your sugar in it and maybe you won't have enough money to buy any more."

They would have so many needs, our new friends. We cannot answer all of them. We must be very faithful to live in all its depth and breadth the little part that God has entrusted to the Fraternity. We must be truly a sign.

Whatever our people are waiting for, it is "Jesus whom we bring and whom they most need." May we master their language quickly to be able to put it into words, but may our daily actions signify already what we are: little, and sisters, and of Jesus.

Brother René Page writes:

When Brother Charles set out alone on an original path, he wasn't driven by a desire for novelty or for doing something different from everybody else. He had a specific way of loving Jesus and it led him, as it turned out, to new things. For our part too, it seems to me, when we started going out to work at ordinary jobs, it wasn't for the sake of making a bang. It was in a desire for real poverty and to follow Jesus more closely. Our bold steps must always spring from this source, and we will need more of them if we're to explore the path of our religious life all the way. It's a path that love alone could have invented, and it's up to love to go on and confirm it today. The path isn't mapped out in advance because it's neither the monastery nor the apostolic life. Contemplative life in the midst of the world once used to be the affair of exceptional beings like St. Benedict Labre and St. Catherine of Siena. And we are not exceptional beings. It is the privilege of Brother Charles to have opened the path. And his heritage is our guide still. I don't say that our love could ever compare with his, but I mean to remind you of the object of his love: Jesus of Nazareth, with the humility, the poverty and the utter lowliness of His life as Savior.

No more than Brother Charles did, can we dissociate Jesus from the men He came to save. The humble realism of the life of Nazareth is clear evidence already how respectfully the Son of God became one of us. And if we want to love as Jesus loved us, words and feelings will not be enough. It will take actions that involve our whole lives. We'll have to make changes that cut deep in ourselves, and that in its own way will testify in whom and in what we have put our hope. For us, as for Jesus, it will be a matter of poverty among men without seeking for guarantees or security. It will be a matter of manual work and humility without side-stepping all the silence and hiddenness of life that can come with them. And it will mostly be a matter of going all the way because it's our life taken as a whole that will bear witness to how true our love is.

We will be faced with the wretchedness and the needs of men, the breadth and variety of which are matched only by the breadth and variety of sin. We have to know that words and generosity are not enough. We possess no means for delivering ourselves from evil. Outside the power of Jesus' sacrifice, there is no salvation for us, still less any hope for a better, more human world. Without the healing of hearts spoiled by sin, or without the new strength of grace, men's good will and their human means will always fall short. Isn't that one of the cruel lessons our own era teaches us?

What is asked of us as Little Brothers is to join the sufferings of men to the sacrifice of Jesus. To be truly offered, these sufferings only lack the miracle of union that the love between Jesus and men accomplishes. It is to such an offering that we are called, and humbly so, for we are only men and no better than the others, no better armed in front of poverty and suffering than they. What is asked of us is the simple courage to take on ourselves, out of love for Jesus and our brothers, what so many others do out of necessity or out of love for their own kind.

A Little Brother of Jesus Writes from Tazrouk,
A Tiny Village of Tuaregs in the Algerian Sahara:

Abdallah, the brother working in the little dispensary is swamped these days. Lots of people are sick. And the customs here for taking care of sick people can sometimes complicate things for a doctor. When there are folks sick in the village, it's a duty for everybody to go visit them, no matter how serious the illness is. When you get up in the morning, you ask who was sick last night and you go and visit them. The "visiting rounds" can last hours. That's why those who are sick are most often put in the largest room of the house in order to receive their visitors. When we're sick ourselves, we find the stream of visits exhausting. But our friends never complain when it happens to them. This way if they should die of their illness, they won't die alone. Abdallah tries never to send anyone to the faraway hospital, and it's not always easy to treat someone seriously ill in a room packed with people whom it would be bad manners to ask to leave. When he brings the patient a fortifying medicine that looks good, the rules of hospitality require that the visitors take a taste of it first and as often as not they finish it up before it gets to the sick person. No matter, the gesture itself is seen as a source of blessing for the house. Science is not everything.

In our room for guests at the fraternity, there are two women just now. They came with a man six days by camel for medical treatment. In a few days a lot of nomads will be coming to the village too. They come and camp with a family of the village to get some of the fruits of the gardens, for it's May now. Hospitality makes sharing normal. Each nomad has a place he always stays, and a certain number of them have gotten into the habit of "squatting" with us. It gives us a chance to stay in contact with these men of the desert, men so totally human. Then we find friends when we go to visit them and are received as their guests in turn.

Most of the men who had left the village to hire on with construction projects are back now. They've come to spend the summer "out of the sun" and with their families. Many will go back to working in their gardens during the summer. But mainly they'll go back to another rhythm of life, a rhythm where work and production yield to the value of "living together." It doesn't bother them at all to take several months of vacation a year. What a difference from a co-worker at the factory in France I remember. He was 35 when he finally took a Sunday off for the first time because he had at last paid off his car. Here people are not slaves to work even if they know how to suffer to earn their living.

The other day a man told me, "I can work all day long in my garden, I won't be tired. But if I do just two hours of work on the construction crew and then the rest of the day I sneak off and sleep, I'll be tired all the same." I think there's a deep truth in what he meant. On a project run by the state or a big company you're caught up in another civilization. You're working for a faceless "government," doing a job you don't always understand, putting in your hours and trying to earn as much as possible while working as little as possible. All that is dehumanizing, and therefore tiring.

In the winter I worked on a construction crew too. I was sharing a life like the other men of our villages: camp-life far from their families. Our base was 250 miles north of Tamanrasset with the team taking measurements and laying out the new asphalt Trans-Sahara Highway. It was a small base with only 40 or so of us. Half were young Algerian technicians from the North — surveyors to trace the route and laboratory technicians to analyze the soil and look for rock deposits along the way that could be used for building. The other half was made up of Algerians from the South, including a certain number of Tuaregs. Between them they did the heavy labor, the driving, and the cooking. I was among the southerners, living in big tents with them, while the northerners lived in cabins. I felt at home and at ease in the desert and with Tuaregs, while the men from the north didn't.

My job was to drive one of the work crews out to the site each day in a landrover. Once there I rarely had time on my hands because there were always little trips here and there to make. Besides, when the camp's reservoir was empty, I had to get water with the tanker truck. I went for water an average of once a week. At the beginning water was 130 miles away, but as the work went on we moved the camp twice and we ended up only 10 miles from a well. It was a good job for me my first time in a camp, without many skills.

Right away I felt at ease in this rugged life, side by side with my co-workers 24 hours a day. I had no corner of my own and my life was all open to them. I matched the rhythm of my prayer to the rhythm of my Moslem comrades. Lauds at daybreak while they turned toward the rising sun. Vespers when we came back from a day's work as the sun was setting. Compline when they were reciting their last prayers. When I was tempted to go to bed without praying, an old laborer beside me in the tent called me back to order. During the day I had time to read a passage of the Gospel, and sometimes a newspaper. In the evening I went off a ways into the desert to have time with the Lord alone.

The rest of the evening we would spend in conversations around the fire. The young northerners would often join us under the tents and we would drink desert tea together. Pleasant gatherings, where my horizons were broadened beyond Tazrouk. There was a good feeling among everybody. You didn't even hear much of that crude language typical in a group of men alone. And yet this desert life was harsh, especially for the northerners who counted the days till their next time off (two weeks' leave after a month and a half of straight work). But work in the South paid double for them, and anyhow I admired how conscientiously they did their jobs.

As for me, I felt myself fully in my place as a little brother. I've often noticed that our life has almost no special signs to mark it. What do our three vows mean in the midst of men celibate by the force of things, who have no other pleasures available than to come sit under the tent and drink tea together? Yet they know that for my part this is a life I've chosen in complete freedom. As for the "sign" of Gospel charity, there was not much margin for me to exercise it. The only thing to do was live with intensity the gift of myself to God in faith in the value of a life that Jesus too chose to live for 30 years at Nazareth.

Now I am back to the village and the fraternity again. In the 15 years we've been here no other new people have ever moved here to stay. It's as if life with the "kel-Tazrouk" seems too demanding to newcomers, for you can't live here without being obliged to live together.

In this context you can understand how much our faith can be a subject of suffering. Our friends worry about it. "It's so many years they've been living among us, sharing our joys, our sorrows and even our prayer sometimes, and they're not Moslems yet." And they're troubled, though perhaps only at the surface of their minds, for God alone can judge the depths of hearts. But it means that in this communal life of the village, we're deeply alone in a way, and the life within us is really a hidden life. All they know of Christianity is what is written about it in the Koran. We're obliged to live apart from them the deepest parts of our friendship as brothers and our friendship with the Lord. That too, everybody in the village doesn't always understand. That's why our hermitage in the desert where we can go for a time of prayer each month is something vital.

Deep mystery, the destiny of these men who don't know the Savior of the world. We know that "the work of God is to believe in the One whom he sent,"[3] and we know that there is no salvation for us outside of that. And yet we believe — the Gospel, the Spirit, and the Church all tell us — that these hundreds of millions of men who don't know "the One whom God sent" will not be lost just for that. Just as we know well that the fact of being baptized and knowing Christ "officially" is absolutely no guarantee that we'll be first in the Kingdom. But then, did God need to go through with the extraordinary adventure of becoming man to save us? If it was to remain unknown to the majority of men, couldn't He have found other means, easier ones? You can understand that Jesus could have been tempted in the desert and in the Garden of Olives to adopt another way of doing things, seemingly more effective, a way that the people around and Satan were pushing Him to take. And yet it was no joking matter that He loved us. We believe that what He did, He did well; and we guess that it all betrays an unimaginable love. No, I don't want to refuse this unfathomable mystery that gives a meaning to my life. I want only to learn to know this Jesus (to know Him with my whole being) so as to be able to live mysteriously from His mystery, if only, by His Spirit, He is pleased to lead me into it.

Your brother,
Taher

From some of the Little Sisters of Jesus in Argentina:

Buenos Aires,
Little Sisters Rolanda and Amalia write:

Why in this city of 9 million did we choose the neighborhood of Monte Chingolo? Because Brother Charles said, "Choose by preference the poorest, those to whom no one else would go." This "villa" (shanty town) in Monte Chingolo was the one where social workers of the zone told us they had given up all activity because the people don't respond, are too passive, and so on. We found an unoccupied lot and in a few weeks with the help of Little Brother Jean Claude we built our "rancho" in the style of the others out of tar paper with a few sheets of zinc for the roof. The day before Christmas Eve, December 23, we started to live in it — amid a hail of bullets with the sound of bombs and machine guns, because just that particular evening a big group of guerillas had attempted to seize the arsenal located 300 yards from us. It would be a fatal night for many teenage boys. The fact of sharing that tragic night with all our neighbors linked us from the beginning, and helped us know for ourselves the seriousness of the situation in the country.

The "villa" extends the length of an old railroad spur, with shanties two or three rows deep. There are several faucets where you can get water and places to connect up to the city electricity. It's rather difficult to estimate the number of families: 150 to 200 at most, the majority of them from the interior of Argentina or from Paraguay.

Several reflections that the children made revealed the questions it raised when we came to live in the villa. "They must have committed some serious crime to be sent here." Others waited to see when we would set up catechism classes for the children. How could they guess that we had come just to share their life?

And now as the years have gone by, the fraternity has become simply part of things. People consider it the place where you can come any time of day and where the little sisters will receive you, listen, help out if need be. The fraternity is a meeting place where folks talk over what's going on in the neighborhood, where we celebrate an occasion, often to the accompaniment of a guitar. They come too to pray together sometimes, for our neighbors are a deeply religious people, though they live practically outside the official Church. They are not at ease in the parish church and feel intimidated in front of the other parishioners who express themselves so easily. It's in the context of their own "villa" that they'll be able to discover that they too are the Church, and we try to make the fraternity a place for this experience.

The situation of the country gets worse day by day. The most recent coup hasn't brought any changes we can see. Violence mounts swiftly, confusion is greater and greater, and life too, harder and harder. Each of us does several hours a week as a housemaid, hoping that one day one of us might be able to work in a factory. But these are times of unemployment, not hiring.

But people have an irrepressible capacity for hope. A few months ago a group of neighbor men resolved to do something to improve the villa. They launched into cementing over the unused railroad spur to make a real street among the houses, so that when it rains there will be a place to walk without sinking in the mud. What pride for all who had worked on it when it was done. And yet it hadn't been an easy effort, for the general atmosphere of the country doesn't promote solidarity.

Villa Ocampo, Little Sister Elena Mercedes writes for the 3 of them there:

It's not easy to tell in a letter what makes up an uneventful, day-to-day life. It's not for nothing that the Gospel tells little about Jesus' life at Nazareth. Yet we want so much to share with you our joy at starting at last this "golondrina" fraternity with the migrants here in the north of Argentina, where we've wanted to be for such a long time.

In a poor continent, an impoverished one, we wanted to meet the extreme situations by a life which shouts the Gospel, not with extraordinary things, but in the ordinary life of those called the "golondrinas." The life of a migrant worker is hard here, for he follows the harvests. That's why he's called a golondrina, a "swallow." With living conditions often inadequate and most of the time inhuman, in houses and lands he's a stranger to, the golondrina is always subject to rain, sun, sickness, without protection and often under great injustice. Last year the profit margin between grower and worker was four to one. This year it is ten to one, and the cost of living is increasing at a startling rate. Because of their no-madic life, golondrinas are always far from the city, with no possibilities of medical help or school for their children. Since last year, we've been sharing the life, the work, the prayer and the hopes of these cotton pickers, so as to live there with Jesus the mystery of Nazareth.

In this region of northeast Argentina, the year is divided into two rather prolonged harvests, cotton and sugar cane. When the harvests are good, the jobs follow one after the other and the families move along with the harvests. The employers aren't the same, and sometimes it's a hundred miles or more between the cotton fields and the cane fields. After two years of picking cotton side by side with the same families, this year we began working in the sugar cane. It wasn't easy to get hired because some thought it wasn't a job for women. Yet several of the other women here with us have been doing it since childhood. The way we finally got hired the first year in the cane was to go in with another family we had worked the cotton har-vests with. They lent us a room of their cabin and we built a little chapel room onto it with the help of the other workers, and also of the employer. The Eucha-rist is there, center of our lives. If we have made ourselves friends of those whom others leave aside, it is because Jesus is their friend. What counts is not so much that we are here, but that because of us Christ is present here.

We know well that three cotton harvests and one of sugar cane make only the very first beginnings of getting to know "golondrina" life. We have lots of miles to travel and lots of things to learn. And what is still ahead of us is surely the most beautiful.

From Brother René Voillaume:

The particular vocation of the Little Brothers of the Gospel is a way of putting into practice another original idea of Father de Foucauld's. At Beni-Abbes and then especially at Tammanrasset, Brother Charles perceived that the work of evangelization of the Tuaregs was inseparable from a minimum of human development. He expressed it by a great respect for all the naturally good human values, by an equal respect for the liberty of men and for the patient work of God in their hearts, and finally by the conviction that a Christian moral and religious life could only be born and grow on the basis of a balanced human life evolving toward progress. That is why Brother Charles had such a constant and attentive interest in all the initiatives that might improve the material, economic, social and family life of the Tuareg tribes. In Brother Charles this deeply understanding and friendly attitude toward others — whoever they might be, Christian or not — was in no way opposed to the conviction that for the others, as for himself, Jesus is the supreme and only Good. Far from it, his attitude was the fruit of divine charity. This charity worked in him a great unity and was the source of a true liberty with regard to all creation. His way of approaching the apostolate, like the basis of his contemplative life, sprang from a single, great love for human nature as God made it, and as the Savior restored it. He saw man's supernatural destiny not as if it was alien or added on to human nature, but as penetrating it and sanctifying it in all its manifestations. This optimistic view of man is profoundly evangelical. It is rooted, in its contemplative expression as in its apostolic manifestation, in an immense and respectful love for men just as they are. In the heart of Brother Charles this love is truly the reflection of the love that animated the heart of the Son of Man for the poorest of His brothers, those the farthest away from Him through ignorance or through the weakness of sin.

The vocation of evangelizing poor people, which is that of the Little Brothers of the Gospel, is deeply marked by this quality of the charity of Brother Charles of Jesus. In the diverse activities of evangelization and of service to which they devote themselves, they must take care that the love they express is the Lord's own love. They must take care not to separate the supernatural life from its human base. They must have a love full of mercy and understanding, respect for all that is good and true in the life of men, respect for the free workings of grace. That means they must be patient and disinterested in the seeking of efficacy, though love requires them to desire to be efficacious in transmitting the true good to men. They'll go as far as they possibly can to place themselves on the level of friendship. The truth of their love demands that they remain attentive to the concrete condition of men and to their most humble needs, for each of these men is greatly loved by Christ.

Fraternity of Little Brothers of the Gospel at Mayo-Ouldemey, Cameroons:

The weather is splendid just now, here in the mountains, by which I mean it rains a lot. Everybody is happy, the millet is growing well, and we hope for a good harvest. August is the month of the year when it rains the most. In two or three months there is as much precipitation here as during the whole year in Paris, I'm told. That tells you that we get some good showers.

Our life at present is quite taken up with the work in the fields. The various evening meetings are set aside for the moment. People are in the fields from morning till night these three months from June to August and are too tired to have meetings in the evening. We'll start them up again soon. What's the work like? It's a group affair: somebody who owns fields prepares millet beer for such and such a day, he invites his neighbors and friends to weed his fields that day, and in the evening, we all drink beer at his house. The next day it's in somebody else's fields, and so it continues. There are easily 20 or 30 men who gather for the work, sometimes more if it's the fields of someone "important," and the tone is always very lively and gay. On other days we go to help somebody or other out in his field, somebody who needs a hand, or a friend, or somebody we'd like to get to know. When you spend the whole day together working like that, you often have a chance to talk, and there are interesting conversations. There are other days when I work in the peanut fields, and another brother, Kloda, too, and it's rare that we're alone working there either. Somebody or another often comes to lend a hand. Sometimes I stay at the fraternity to rest or for language study or translating the Gospel. Or to write to you, like today.

And little by little through it all, who knows how, Christ is proclaimed, eyes open, mentalities change. The parable of the mustard seed or the "grain that grows of itself"[4] comes out in a special way here, for truly what we do for people and what we try to tell them with our stumbling use of their language and lots of clumsy moves is no great thing. But we marvel to see that some of them understand and succeed in translating into their own way of thinking and into their daily lives at Madas, Guendeleys, and Oulde-meys this Gospel that we're trying to hold out to them. Our role as little brothers here is tending to become the role of ones who retire into the background, and I'm glad about it. More and more they are the ones who take the initiatives and make the decisions as to holding meetings, leading the liturgy, sharing out the "goods" of all sorts, undertaking communal work projects, and so on. And our role more and more in the background is also more and more essential: our place is to be present, to offer discreet suggestions as to what lies within the Gospel path, by a word, a gesture, an action — and above all by our life of prayer which we desire to become deeper and deeper. Our role is likewise the example of being united as brothers the way we live among ourselves.

As I speak about our more and more hidden role as little brothers, I could point out too the importance in our life of whatever sufferings and hardships come our way, and the gift of humiliation that we receive from the hand of the Lord. We are never short of such things, as you know, and it is a source of life for these groups of people we are trying to aid. Thus it is that the whole of our lives as little brothers becomes apostolic.

And so, little communities of "believers" are created here and there, at Mayo-Ouldemey and in several villages in the plains region that we go to visit. These communities are at different stages. There are catechumens, (André is the brother more specially concerned with them), "companions in prayer," (pre-catechumens), and those who begin to be attracted. All I can give you is a glimpse. How can you get an accurate idea of these little groups springing up here or there? I'll tell you about one of these little communities getting started in the area of the plain that I go to visit, at Memey. I've been going to Memey for 5 or 6 years and for a long time nothing seemed to happen, but now it looks like something is growing. They already believe in Jesus, but they aren't baptized yet, or even catechumens, except for one. This one who's a catechumen got things started. Every Sunday he travels the 10 miles to come here to the liturgy in the morning, and around him at Memey there grew up a little community that gathers at his house every Sunday evening for a liturgy of the Word which he leads. From time to time I attend. After the liturgy we gather with some of the "companions in prayer" from the group and we reflect together on the problems that come up for these people who are at the very beginnings of their Christian life and desire to go further: the problem of getting married and starting a family with a little love in it, the problem of relations with the Moslems they live among (a problem that occupies us brothers too), clashes with the fairly numerous Adventists around and with their own families who don't always understand them. All of them want to go further and to reach the point of being fully members of the Christian family, but all of them are quite aware that there is a long road in front of them, and an important one.

The other day, as one of the members of this group had been sick for a while, they made a decision at the meeting and carried it out a few days later: to go and work in his field for no charge.

In their Sunday evening discussions my role is discreet too. I prefer to let them talk things out and find solutions themselves. Besides they speak Mandara, the lingua franca of the Moslems of the region, and I don't understand this language. To follow the conversation I get one to translate from time to time for me into Ouldemey and then I try to slip in the little word that will help them go further. I admit that this work that consists of getting a little community of believers started and watching its beginnings is a work that thrills me.

If they speak Mandara in the group it's because it's quite a mixed one: Ouldemeys, Maktaleys, Hursos, Zulgos, Muyans, Podokos, and Madas. The fraternity first came to the region for the Madas and the Ouldemeys in the mountains, but for a good while it's been no longer limited exclusively to them, for on the plains all the tribes mingle.

I've only told you a small part, but maybe you've been able to share a little bit, as I hoped, not the problems of Mayo-Ouldemey, but our life and our day-to-day joys. The chief problem you know: who will be the priests who take in charge the little Church that is beginning here? The ideal situation is to wait for priests and deacons from the community itself, or rather to foster them and help with their formation. Meantime we will try to fill the gap. Perhaps it won't be long till our role is finished here.

Jowotona, Venezuela,
The Little Sisters of the Gospel write:

There are two Indian tribes here in this region of the forest, the Makiritaris and the Sanemas. We wanted to bring the Gospel to them all, but it was clear that we had to begin by winning the friendship of the Makiritaris, for they are the ones who navigate the river and have absolute control over the access to the region. Now at last we can turn toward the Sanemas too, all the while going on and deepening our friendship with the Makiritaris. The Lord is sending us to the two tribes: may all one day know the infinite tenderness of the Father for them.

And the Lord said:

"I have seen the affliction of my people; truly I know their sorrow. And I mean to deliver them."[5]

We're helping our Sanema friends discover their possibilities for the future so that they'll perhaps be able little by little to take their economic and cultural independence. But how can they achieve it? There are still years to wait.

Last year in August we started to teach the Sanemas to read and write, teenagers and adults. We had some difficulties at the beginning because some of the Makiritaris, who have always been the ruling tribe, reacted. But now the Sanemas themselves have organized a part of their camp into a little "school." One of them took charge of teaching his own group to read, while we follow the progress of another group. This group too has already chosen one of themselves to be in charge.

We'd like to go and live in their camps to share their life from closer up. The Sanemas are still very much nomads and live above all from hunting and gathering. But there are some who are starting to plant manioc and bananas. If we lived with them, we could get together for meetings after work is done, to talk things out. We want to help them become aware of their situation and of the situation of all ethnic minorities, and through it give them an opening on the whole world. But we have a lot to do to catch onto their language.

I told you already we felt called to deepen our

friendship with the Makiritaris. Yes, we must become more and more a part of the Makiritari community where we live. That explains our efforts to join in all the more with tribal life. In particular we've taken the garden work quite to heart, the way a Makiritari woman does. We're going to have a new plot this year. That's an important event in the life of a woman of the forest. The time of sowing is a privileged moment of sharing.

Garden work is not the only women's job, as you other little sisters who've spent years in the jungle can testify. You can't forget to go cut wood regularly, make the cazaba bread from manioc roots, fetch water, go fishing and all the rest that's part of daily life.

Now that two lay volunteers have come to take charge of the Makiritari children's school, we can give ourselves more to helping the adults learn to read. We get together in the evening after work. These meetings with the adults often lead to some good dialogues.

To our joy, we've been able to begin a real collaboration with one of the Makiritari men on the promotion of the people. He himself proposed to gather everybody in the atta (the men's roundhouse) so that all can say what they think and together, as a community, reflect on specific topics that he offered to choose himself.

We really do feel that our Ye'cuana friends consider us as one of their family, one of their community. We can't forget what effort and hardships it cost the brothers and sisters who lived here before us to bring to birth this ever deepening friendship within which we live among them, sharing intensely their sorrows, their toil and their joys too.

We're aiming directly at helping our Makiritari

friends to find their bearings in relation to the outside world still unknown to most of them. As we talk together, we often use the aid of charts and pictures to explain their situation in the context of Venezuela and the rest of Latin America. It's a way for them to get to know people all across the world who are victims of war, oppression and hatred.

And then in the midst of this situation of injustice between the two tribes, the Makiritaris and the Sanemas whom they press into their service, we try to help the Makiritaris realize what their faith requires of them. During a liturgy, after the reading of the text of James 2 on the respect due to the poor and the Gospel passage on Lazarus and the rich man, one of the Christians denounced publicly and vigorously that attitude of superiority that Makiritaris often have toward their Sanema brothers. It was the first time. Surely the Spirit had given him light. The more they become possessed by the Spirit, the more they will be witnesses of Love in the midst of their brother tribesmen in whose ways it's often might that makes right.

"To say God is to say love."

And we? How are we doing in this attitude of respect toward each one of our friends? Do we always know how to excuse their reactions that sometimes take us aback, or is there a dose of superiority and even harshness mingled in with our ways? When we look at each one of them with the eyes of Christ, what do we discover? We often discover beings who feel crushed, as if they were swamped by everything around them. They themselves have a sense of inferiority often deep-rooted and we too easily would forget it. So then how humbly we must look on them.

Yes, our task must always be to hold out our hand expressing to them all the tender care of Wanaadi, God who loves them.

Little Sister Magdeleine of Jesus writes:

To be a Savior with Jesus and to "cry his Gospel by your life," you must be ready to leave your family, background, country, language, customs, way of thinking, and all you hold dear. You will then be able to belong to those you have been sent to by making your own their language, customs, and even their mentality, however different from yours they may be.

You must become completely one with your new people. Just wanting to love is not enough, for you must become one with them in all the hard realities of life.

And no one, absolutely no one, must be excluded from your love. You must not forget those who are hardest to reach, in countries and in situations that seem impenetrable or hostile.

You should choose to live among the poorest and most forgotten, "where no one else would go": among nomads or other ignored or disregarded minorities. Look at the map of the world and see if you can find a handful of people scattered over a large territory and difficult to reach for those with a different form of apostolate. You must really choose to go there, otherwise no one else may ever come to tell them that Jesus loves them, that He suffered and died for them.

On the day of your religious profession, you will offer your life in self-sacrifice united with Jesus on the cross, for the sake of the people of Islam among whom Brother Charles gave his life, and for the whole world. You will renew your universal offering every day at Mass, but this will not keep you from loving faithfully the people who have become yours by adoption. Jesus died to save all the people of the world, yet He too chose a certain people and lived, suffered and died among them. Your love must be so strong that you too will be able to give your life in joy in union with the sacrifice of Christ on the altar who died to redeem all men.

Brother Charles will speak to you of this love that leads to immolation. He will ask you to desire, in total submission to the Will of God, the highest of graces, martyrdom, so that like Jesus you may give the greatest proof of love. More than all else, he will ask you to die to yourself in sacrifice day after day, hour after hour, in what your daily life will ask of you, which is the hidden immolation everyone can attain.

The Little Sisters of Jesus Tell
Of One of Their Fraternities in Alaska:

Little Diomede — a tiny dot on the map — is a small island on the Alaskan side of the Bering Strait, 2.6 miles from the Siberian Island, Big Diomede. In two hours we can walk around our island's cliffed shore when the sea is frozen.

You might ask yourself why this little place would have an importance? Why do people love it? What can make living there worthwhile?

For twenty years we little sisters have been living on this rock for several months each year with twelve Eskimo families, sharing their daily life. A hundred people living closely together become more like a large family, everyone working together and helping each other, and we became part of it.

You probably wonder how we live our days. It's a life quite different from San Francisco or New York, but where each small event has its importance, each person being very important and unique in the eyes of God.

There are some great values to be found in Eskimo life and a very highly specialized culture which they had to develop in order to survive on the very fringe of the habitable earth. Sharing is one of the keys to survival in the Arctic. Selfishness has no place in the existence of man in these regions, and every day brings many proofs of this.

Take a day in May when we felt our little house (15 by 20 feet) shaken all night by violent winds. We knew another day of heavy snow was in view. For a week now we had not been able to see Big Diomede. While we were having breakfast, one of the men knocked at the door to see how we were doing, to "check on us," as he usually says jokingly, with a big smile of brotherly concern. He and his brother have killed many polar bears in their life with only a knife before the time of rifles — a dangerous hunt done only by the bravest. His experience and deep knowledge told him this kind of weather could not change in an hour or two. "No plane today," was his tranquil statement, although the village had been waiting for the mail bush-plane for over a month now. It might not come at all, as the ice between the two islands where the planes land was threatening to break up. And then he would not receive the new part for his outboard motor necessary for the walrus hunting. Patience and endurance are part of the great wisdom of the Arctic. Never to make any definite plans and to make the best of any situation are the beautiful secrets to be understood and learned. Any newcomer would soon be won over by the Eskimos' impressive serenity and calmness, and trade his worries for the typical attitude of "We'll do it weather permitting," that leaves everything in the hands of God.

One of our neighbors would come over a little later. She was worrying about our "naluait," bleached seal skin which must dry while frozen. That year a rise in temperature made it difficult and she was sorry to hear that we had lost the larger of our two skins which was blown away by a strong wind. Out of generosity she told us to come and get a piece of her naluait if we should need it. Yet she had very little for their own sewing. She would also give Little Sister Clara good advice on how to sew her sealskin slippers since it was her first year on the island. When each of us first came, we were taught this art too, as well as stretching and scraping skins for tanning. Any one of our friends is always happy and ready to explain their way of living and the techniques they have developed to be able to survive in this rugged environment.

Fishing and crabbing through the ice are other vital skills. Hunting is the men's work but cutting up the seals and storing away the meat are the women's jobs. The skins must be removed without spoiling them. Although we were unskilled, the people trusted us to try when they realized we were eager to learn. Their warm and simple hospitality made us feel at home right away.

When it is stormy, no one goes out unless it is necessary — to get water for instance. A village water tank has been installed, but it doesn't work yet, so we still have to cut a chunk of clean snow from the hillside above the houses and carry it down a slippery slope. A newcomer usually falls every third step, and of course, loses the block of snow which breaks into pieces. Then the next thing to do is climb up and get another one.

The good side of these long stormy days is that we are able to do more sewing. By evening we were happy to have completed sewing a pair of sealskin pants for a widower in the village and also to have some slippers to sell at the store. This small store also buys ivory and while we were there a young boy was selling an ivory bracelet and a bird he had made. Walrus ivory is the main source of income. The Diomeders are known as some of the best carvers, learning the trade very young. Their most beautiful and unusual pieces of art are sold on the outside market, bearing their signatures.

In the evening several men were looking at the sky and predicted that it would clear up. Sure enough the next morning the sky was blue and the sun was shining. It was one of those days when everything seemed to happen at once. We climbed to the two top houses of the village to return an Eskimo yoyo pattern and a tool we had borrowed. There we learned it was safe to go crabbing. So we set out for the ice, chopped holes, and lowered our lines. We came home with several big crabs.

On the radio we heard that a plane was coming, so we wrote some letters because we knew that it would probably be the last plane before the ice broke up. We also helped a young mother with her laundry as she was sick, and later on when her husband came back with two seals from hunting, she called us to help her again.

The plane came and what a joy to receive mail! Although the news was not too recent, we were happy just the same. For world news everyone has a radio, and just last year a telephone was installed on the island. It has made a big difference for everyone.

We shared some of our crabs with a blind lady friend. One of our little neighbors came with a dish of walrus flippers, a delicacy his mother had cooked and wanted to share. He was followed by his father, who wanted to make sure we were back from crabbing as the ice was becoming unsafe. And as we were about to begin our time of prayer together that evening, we heard a voice on the porch saying, "the plane sure made it just in time!" So we joined everyone gathered outside to watch in awe the sudden breaking of the ice swept away by the current.

As soon as the ice breaks, the great walrus hunt begins. This is the biggest event of the year. Three skin boats and their crews would go after the walruses, work throughout the "night" ("night" as bright as day because of the midnight sun), sleep only a few hours, and start again.

We always receive a large share of fresh meat, and each family wants us to consider their meat storage hole as our own. Each year we spend long hours working hard with the women on the beach preparing the huge walrus hides that are used to remake the skin boats. The blubber has to be removed from the skin and the skin slit thinly in two. Little Sister Josepha was so happy the first time she was entrusted with this job many years ago. The least slip of the knife would make the boat leaky. The seams also have to be sewn in such a way that they are waterproof. These boats are much stronger for the ice floes than any other type of boat.

Summertime also brings millions of migratory birds from Japan, which spend the summer nesting on the rocks of the island. This means fresh eggs for everybody. Besides, we can pick edible greens from between the rocks. It's an explosion of life.

The priest comes only three or four times a year to this tiny village, but on Sundays we all pray together in the little church, thanking God for His blessings and entrusting everyone's cares to Him.

Like Jesus at Nazareth, the one thing we want to bring to our Diomede friends is God's love, our greatest treasure.

Our prayer on this tiny island reaches also to all the people in the world. May we become one big family!

A Little Brother of the Gospel in Benares:

After my novitiate, I was only too eager to begin living the vocation of the Fraternity in my own country. So I found the learning of a local trade one of the first musts. I set out from the fraternity and stopped at random at the first carpentry shop I saw on the road, and there I was accepted as an apprentice. No tools, nor much inquiry about myself. From the very first day I felt as if I were starting a new life. The traditional village schools in India are under the shadow of a tree, and there was I under the new tree, not learning the Vedas like children, nor even just carpentry, but the North Indian way of life itself. Among the few things my co-workers knew about me was that my education had been in English. So they were very proud to teach me Hindi, or rather Bhojpuri, the local dialect. Now I still do not catch all of the conversation, but it is coming.

Though I am an Indian from Goa, for them I am a foreigner, a poor fellow who had to go so far in search of a job. Therefore, especially at the beginning, they took me very much in charge. They even convinced me to prepare meals with them. I was very touched to see how almost everybody wanted to help me and teach me to cook. The standard food in all the province consists of thick unleavened pancakes called rotis which they eat either with a little vegetable sauce or molasses.

The rhythm of work and rest here is special. There is no such thing as a fixed day of rest. They take it when they are invited to a marriage or a funeral meal, when they go for a pilgrimage to worship a famous divinity in a faraway village, or when they are sick. The saying goes that there are seven days in a week and eight feasts in Benares. There are pilgrims who come from the villages around as well as from far places all over India. Every feast is marked by taking a bath in the Ganges, by a devotional visit to a local temple, according to the feast, and by distributing prasad, (the offerings presented at the temple to the deity) to friends and neighbors. The Ganges must surely be a sacrament of the covenant God made with the world. For ages Hindus have believed in its purifying bath. Since Christ took his bath in water and blood, He has summed up all other baths of the world liturgy, it seems to me. That is how I pray when I learn about their feasts and share in them.

To learn the carpenter's trade, I became the disciple of the head of the shop. He is my guru and I am expected to accept everything he says and also to render him every service he may need. I fetch his cigarettes, his food, even water his calf.

Normally the apprenticeship for manual work and trades begins as a young boy. You "see" your father, your neighbor, or your guru "doing." You pick up the tricks of the trade as your guru executes them every day before your eyes. There is little explanation, few words. For instance, for planning the wood there are no promptings such as left, right, slow, fast, hard, gently. The disciple simply follows the movements of the guru. It reminded me of the suppleness required to let ourselves be "led by the Spirit."

When the question of wages came at the end of the first week, great was my humiliation when my guru told me he could pay only one rupee a day, for he considered me like a little apprentice-boy. It was like a reminder that I was being "reincarnated" among a new people.

My workshop is in the open air, under the shadow of a neem tree, a tree famous in India for its shade, on the main road. It is a rather small enterprise. We are eight workers, counting the two owners, who are brothers. Kakanu, who is my guru, is a man of very few words. Plenty of lively jokes. I am always edified at his simplicity and humility. The place where he lives is a little shack. He and his wife live with the barely necessary things. He owns only one loin cloth and one hurta (a long shirt), no shoes or sandals. Just one dish and one cup for both. Of course here this is not a problem, for the wife eats after she has served the husband. I have learned a lot from Kakanu, from the way full of respect in which he addresses the customers, besides the many tricks of the trade, big and little, which you can learn only by watching for many days the way the guru does.

There is a complicated set of customs for ritual purity. It was not easy to be told at first that much of my behavior was impure. For example, to be in a state of purity, one has to wash his hands, feet, and mouth before and after meals. And since they have seen us brothers eat on our way to work, or while cooking at the fraternity (even just tasting) in the eyes of our neighbors we are likely to be at any time in a state of impurity. That's why one of our neighbors once told us that nobody could accept something to eat from our hands. A hard thing to be told.

It surprises me that some find it easier to adopt new concepts of thinking at the intellectual level among Hindu people, than to adopt new patterns of everyday behavior. I do not have the right to dismiss these patterns as irrational. Respecting them is a part of the descending that constitutes the mystery of the Incarnation in its divine "foolishness." Gradually I understand that I have to respect the feelings of these people who have become my own, to be able to love them and come near to them. I have to do like them to be reborn among them.

Caste is perhaps the most delicate issue in North India. "To which caste do you belong?" It was the constant question I had to face in the beginning. I answered simply that I belonged to the humankind. Right from the beginning I understood that I had to be uncompromising on this point, and that it was here that my witness and sharing of the Good News could begin. Sometimes I tried to say that those who believe in Jesus should make no distinction among men, that Jesus loves all men, and that He died for all. I don't think they understood it. I will simply have to live it among them.

When I first arrived, they called me a yogi. They thought I must be a Bengali, for Benares has seen many refugees from East Bengal who have settled here.

For Easter Triduum I took three days off. Among the other news the local radio announced that April 16 was Good Friday for Christians. So when

I came back my co-workers asked me if I was a Christian. I had not introduced myself to them that way at first so that they would not stick labels on me. To be a Christian in the mentality of North Indian Hindus is to have a link with the institutions of the Church and her influence, such as schools, hospitals, and so forth, which live on foreign aid. It suggests colonial powers, missionary activity and conversions. Now the turning point has come, and among the people of my carpentry shop I must find the discreet and patient ways that go at their own rhythm:

— to announce Jesus and not myself.
— to announce a mystery, not my history.
— to live day by day just as I am with both my defects and qualities, without having to justify a label.
— to love and serve much, to become a friend and brother.

Your brother,
Vishwas

From the Writings of Brother René Voillaume:

If the inner life of a little brother must be filled with the love of God, you can say that his exterior actions and his entire way of living must be wholly inspired by the friendship that he has for men. It is difficult for the immense majority of men to believe that God shows them a personal interest. Evil, suffering and death form a screen between men and God and make it difficult to perceive the mystery of love hidden in God. Yet never have men needed so badly to believe in the divine friendship toward them, and not merely a sort of general, impersonal love in which God would enfold his creatures all together.

The love of God for each one is a friendship full of tender affection, which calls each one by his name. How can one manage to believe in it? Even the sufferings Jesus endured, His agony and His death, (which are, as you might say, God's last try to make us understand) don't always manage to convince hearts when the evil and the wretchedness of their lives have left them disillusioned, indifferent, or in a state of revolt.

How can you teach the faith to a man who has not at least begun to suspect that he is loved with a love of friendship by God? The task of the fraternities is that men may believe in the reality of the friendship God bears toward them. Without this preparation of hearts, how could they perceive the proof of love through the narrative of the passion of Jesus? A man, especially one who has been hardened by too heavy a work, too much injustice, too great a poverty, needs, before he can believe in love, to discover a clear manifestation of it. The little brothers must be for such men the manifestations of this gratuitous love.

The life of little brothers must first of all demonstrate that they believe for themselves in this immense love of their God. Their voluntary poverty, the time consecrated to prayer before the Blessed Sacrament, the peace, the joy, their consecrated chastity, will be signs that the little brothers believe themselves loved by Jesus. There is a way of believing in Christ's friendship for you, in how great and faithful it is, that is transparent in your life. Likewise, the brothers' lives have to show that they believe in Christ present in the Church and its teachings.

Do not forget that the first sign by which men are to recognize the presence of a divine friendship will be the genuine love that we will have for one another.

This point is so vital that the absence of fraternal love would ruin the apostolic work of a community. Jesus cannot manifest himself through a community divided by lack of love.

Jesus has asked us to love men exactly as He Himself loved them. You could sum up the life of a little brother by saying that he must do everything possible so that his sentiments, his actions, and his way of living become the sentiments of Jesus for men. This mission is so absolute that it must be the guiding principle for every aspect of our life. To love as Jesus loved: to love with a friendship made of infinite respect in a very total and very humble gift of ourselves.

The Little Sisters of Jesus Describe How They Started a Fraternity:

We've dreamed for a long time of a second fraternity in Seoul, a fraternity planted in a poor neighborhood to complete the witness of our regional fraternity here in the capital. Now we've had the joy of realizing our dream. The four new Korean postulants who joined this year made it possible.

Before we started looking, we waited for the harsh Korean winter to be over. We didn't much have the heart to go walking through the very poor neighborhoods before we had really become part of them at the time when life must be very tough. But when spring came, we started looking for a neighborhood that could become ours. For three weeks we went all through Seoul and its surroundings. The city is very spread out and continually growing. It will soon have a population of seven million.

In the past 25 years in a country devastated by

the war, a great deal has been accomplished from the standpoint of housing and repairs. But everything can't be done in a day or even in ten years, especially when the population is young and in full demographic expansion. There are many little streams, tributaries of the River Man, running through Seoul. It's along them that we found the shantytown neighborhoods, some of them right downtown, others near the outskirts. They are built long and narrow, stretched out for several miles but squeezed in between the streams and the well-to-do neighborhoods. Many other such shantytowns are built high, stacked up on the hills in Seoul's wide surrounding area. The hill shantytowns are better aired and less cramped, but there people have the problem of water and coal supplies. Sometimes they have to carry up everything on their backs, a 20 or 30 minute walk. They also have the problem of being far from the city and places of work.

In the city there are three big concentrations of shanty-dwellers: two downtown and one on the outskirts in an industrial zone. We could have pictured a fraternity well in all three of them, but we had to choose and finally we picked the third one, Mok Dong, since the other two are already slated to be torn down, at least on paper.

A shanty for the fraternity was not hard to find. Shacks never stay empty. They're bought and sold on the spot with just a few minutes' reflection and time only for a rapid glance at the interior where people are usually sleeping since many work at night. No deeds to worry about. The neighborhood is illegal. We came one morning to buy a little shack we had spotted a few days before. It was no longer free, and we settled for another one 20 yards farther. The Lord must have been watching because we realized afterwards that it suits us better than the other one would have. They are little shacks, built however somebody could in cinderblocks or boards, sometimes with a thatched roof but most often just tar paper. When the weather is nice the sun fixes things up. When it rains a heart-rending sadness floods the whole neighborhood.

Sunday, April 20, was moving day. It didn't take long for we didn't have much: our homemade furniture, the big bouls (Korean quilts), and plywood sheets to put on the inside walls of the fraternity. As soon as we arrived, a swarm of little boys gather to help us unload the truck. A neighbor lady lends us a broom to start our cleaning, another brings us a big plastic basin so we can make our water supply. The house stays full all day long. By evening we have the impression that we've met half the neighborhood, but it's only an impression. Little by little we discover the density of the population around us. In a twelve yard radius of the fraternity, there are 20 families with children, and often there are young sons-in-law and daughters-in-law living with them too.

We got initiated quickly by our various neighbors into neighborhood life. For the electricity a whole cluster of houses are hooked up to the same meter and the one whose house the meter is in is a grandmother who seems to hold a certain authority in the neighborhood. When each bill arrives, she tries to divide up the total among all the houses according to her judgment. When she sees that the meter shows a big outlay and she'll have a hard time getting people to pay without arguing too much, she cuts off the current.

For three weeks we worked hard from morning to night to fix the fraternity up, especially the chapel. Luckily Soudok, a postulant little brother, could come and help us lay the cement for the floor. We also put a new coat of tar paper on the roof because we had already noticed leaks and the rainy season was coming.

A month after we moved in the vicar general came to say the first Mass and to place the Blessed Sacrament in our chapel. On that day our new house became fully a fraternity. Meantime we had had the great joy of a visit from the cardinal. He had come one Sunday for Confirmation at the parish and he wanted to stop at the fraternity. He stayed a half hour with us and the little room quickly filled up with neighbors and little children who came to see who was there. Right away the rumor had gone out that someone exceptional had arrived in the neighborhood. Everyone loved the cardinal for the kindness of his manner, but he was very moved by the destitution that surrounds us.

Destitution and suffering. The suffering that leaps to your eyes is the one written on the face of each child. There is Ok-Souni the little girl next door, eight years old, whom we found one stormy evening alone with her little brother in their flooded kitchen sitting on a cement ledge and crying silently. Pong-Ha, maybe six years old, with a little face all swollen and blue around her eyes. We asked her what happened and she just shrugged, "Somebody beat me." Who? We didn't even try to find out because it's impossible to condemn anyone for it. If we were in their place in such conditions of housing and tiredness, we would be quite incapable of holding back a gesture of impatience or anger. A few days later Pong-Ha's little brother drowned in a mud-hole very close to the neighborhood. We learned then that their father had committed suicide two years ago. Since then their mother had worked in a factory and it was usually

Pong-Ha who watched her little brother. But those past days she had been very sick. Besides, in all the excitement, nobody thought of her. We took her twice to the hospital for treatments and exams, a lucky thing for her and for everyone as it turned out, for she had typhus.

Opposite the fraternity on the other side of the passage way two little boys, Sou-Hili, six, and Sou-Jougi, four, live with their father who's been a widower for two years. He gets up at 4:30 in the morning, cooks a pot of rice, takes part of it for his meals at work and leaves the rest for the children to come dig into when they get hungry. At 6:00 he leaves for his work as a construction laborer and he comes back at 8:30 at night. The little boys are alone all day. They play in the passageways, or sometimes with arms around each other's shoulders they set out for a walk to see what they can see. When the site where their father is working is not too far away, they try to go find him. Now they always stop by the fraternity. "Little Sister, we're going to see Papa." And when they return, "Little Sister, we're back." It must be good when you feel that in spite of everything you're not absolutely alone in the neighborhood from morning to night.

Tong-Jini is Ok-Pouni's little brother, five years old. Their mother went away a few days before we came to the neighborhood. She just gave up. And so, when his sister goes to school, Tong-Jini is completely alone. What wonder if at the smallest thing he starts to cry? When I think of our neighborhood, it's often the little face of Tong-Jini all smudged with dust or tears I have in front of my eyes, or the face of Pong-Ha which is so hard to make smile. When her mother went away, we were able to reach her grandmother, who lives a bit farther in the same shanty town. She is a Christian and what courage she has. She keeps house for her oldest daughter, a widow who has to work though she has four children. It's a comfort for the grandmother to come into our little chapel and say the rosary with us. But often all she can do is cry. And like her, everybody keeps on with courage, trying to face up to all the misfortunes that sometimes pile one on top of the other. How do they manage not to be bitter?

It was Good Friday the day we went to pay for our little fraternity. For us it was the sign that only the Cross of Jesus would be our light. As we live with our neighbors we penetrate further and further into the mystery of the Lord's Passion, and the Cross of Jesus will help us understand the meaning of their suffering.

From a Little Brother of Jesus in Sao Paolo:

I just came back to Brazil after finishing my theology studies and the preparation for my final vows in the central fraternity in France. I'm almost having to get readapted to my own country. I went to buy something the other day and the shop-keeper told me I speak with an accent. Yet it's good, it gives me a chance not to be so sure of myself and to rediscover my country and values that seem like new.

It's taken me a long time to find a job. In the course of five weeks I went to some 150 different factories (Greator Sao Paolo boasts 4,000 metallurgical plants), starting out early in the morning and coming back to the house in the afternoon. Everywhere there were people — from ten to 1,000 according to the case — standing in front of the factory entrances. Waiting, asking, being turned down every time is humiliating for everyone, and I had to take that too. When you're lucky enough to be allowed inside you have to go through very complicated psycho-technical tests which immediately eliminate the illiterate (56% of our population) and the slow. And if you manage to pass these tests, you still have to be interviewed by a specialist probing into your past, and then have a medical examination. In one factory (General Motors) where there was an opening for a floor-sweeper, they demanded an elementary school diploma and two years of experience in the trade.

The job must have gone to someone more gifted than I was, and I had to continue the hunt, until I had tried 150 plants. I was constantly struck by the equanimity and patience of the job-hunters even when things dragged out for months. It is true that for most people there is yet no explicit awareness that the situation is an abnormal one. Our working class is still rather young by comparison with a capitalism that is a hundred years old and wily. In any case, that good temper kept on impressing me.

Finally one fine day a boy of 16 who works as an office boy in a metallurgical plant asked me to come and try for a job there. Having someone introduce you at such and such a factory is also a way of getting hired. It was the company that makes the clutches for all the cars manufactured at Sao Paolo and was located at Santo Bernardo do Campo, the neighboring town to Santo Andre where the fraternity is. There are other factories too in the same vicinity that often give men coming from the country a chance. No psycho-technical tests, no diplomas required, but only a practical test in front of a machine. So I had to have the look of someone "just arrived" in Sao Paolo. They could tell, though, that I wasn't from the country by the way I took hold of the machine. At the end of an hour or so, I found myself accepted. At last.

At the moment we are around 300 workmen, whereas we were 500 at the beginning of the year. Outside of a few specialized workers, the great majority are the "unskilled" type. The atmosphere is marked by the youth of the majority and by the fact that a good many of us come from other parts of the country. There are many from the North East states. So it was that I was caught in the scuffle like any other man coming from another State.

At the end of three months I became an operator on a machine that is quite easy to work. With a long sort of cogged steel brush it makes grooves on the inside of the hole in the center piece of the brake-plate. It is regulated to groove a piece every eight to 15 seconds. This requires me to make the same motion over and over again through the 9½ hours of the working day, and yet I got accustomed to it all right and now I even like the work.

I produce the required amount of work all right, and even sometimes a little more, but I still draw the minimum pay. This is the first time I have seen even young girls — about 30 of them — in overalls and no less at ease than the men before their machines. The superintendance is very strict so as to prevent the workers from talking too much together, as well as to keep the machines going all the time. It is even carried so far as watching the time people spend in the toilets. Another surprising thing that happened to me was to be stopped from entering the factory because I had picked up in front of the door a paper that turned out to be a notice of a union meeting. The kindly doorman explained that he had to obey an order put out by the management in view of the fact that "that sort of thing came from a bad group of people." Little things like these occur again and again, like reminders that we can always be dismissed at a moment's notice. Many of the workers would like to leave on account of this pressure and the low wages, but we stick to our jobs because it's almost certain we would be unemployed a long time.

I think of something I heard a Little Brother of the Gospel say:

"In a situation of injustice and oppression, thank God for the movements of consciousness-raising and liberation for the poor. There have been days when I've asked myself whether following Jesus at Nazareth was any use or whether it would be better for us to get into the struggle more directly.

"But I think this life of imitating Jesus at Nazareth is a part of the direct struggle. To live a quality of love for the poor people whom we have made our friends, that indicates who God's special friends are and where true riches lie. That lets loose the subversive power of the Gospel. It strikes at the psychological roots of the situations of oppression, a perverted way of thinking that finds it normal that the well-furbished fellow be respected and admired and a poor fellow be disregarded. Those psychological structures are false and our lives have to announce that God doesn't see things that way.

"It's like the brothers said when we were together for our chapter, 'The witness of friendship is already a path of evangelization and a ferment of liberation, for simply looking with love and sensitivity at a poor person, at a person rejected by others, provokes a liberating interior transformation and contains a manifestation of God's love. And besides, this loving look given to someone poor is a testimony to others, for it reveals the greatness and the dignity of those who are considered little and poor.'"

Little Sister Annie, Prioress of
The Little Sisters of Jesus, writes to them:

I'm just back from a tour of the fraternities in Switzerland. Shortly before that I was in France. I cannot forget what I saw a few months ago in the Sahara, in Niger, and again in Latin America, and that is perhaps why I was particularly conscious of the contrast in the way of living as well as in the scenery.

With the green fields and peaceful forest of Switzerland before my eyes, how can I fail to remember the desolate stretches and dried up bushes of the desert? While passing by so many well stocked stores in France, how can I forget our drought-stricken N'Guigmi friends who wait for hours for the daily distribution of millet which will keep them from dying?

How then can we live poor in the heart of a society which is based on the consumption of material goods and submitted to techniques of publicity which tend to destroy personhood more and more?

A fraternity among factory workers in Europe cannot be the same as a tent fraternity among nomads in the Sahara, but our way of life must to a certain extent be a protest against the materialism around us with its drive for comfort and excessive mechanization.

We must protest because of Gospel values. Because man does not live by bread alone, and especially because if all men are our brothers, it is not possible that a minority should endlessly create for itself new and superfluous needs while a vast majority of men lack the minimum.

We must also face up to the danger of inevitable mediocrity if we are not constantly urged on by new appeals to our generosity, like Brother Charles whose whole life was so marked by his single-minded search for God.

We must help each other to remain poor and free with regards to material goods. All the Little Sisters together and each Little Sister personally must feel responsible for the poverty that we have chosen to live, and each Little Sister must begin by living its requirements herself. Remember that in materially-privileged countries too, there is a thirst for the hope that Gospel poverty bears witness to. The modern world has created new forms of impoverishment.

Be a leaven of hope and gratuitous love in a society more and more given over to materialism and a mad race for money and profit. The occidental world must come to a generous understanding of the needs of others and overcome their fears of having to share, thinking they will not have enough for themselves. We must share this grace of universality that has marked us. We must help others to love those whom they would not love spontaneously because of so many prejudices of class, nation, and race.

The Little Brothers of Jesus send news from Their Fraternity in Detroit, U.S.A.:

Bernard:
　　It was early in June when I arrived in Detroit from the studies-fraternity, happy to be back home with my brothers and friends. Our neighbors hadn't

changed much since I left last year. A few more
houses had disappeared, emptied and boarded up or
simply torn down and wiped away by the city's bull-
dozers. Sam with his job at the nearby foundry has
become part of the scenery as he walks with his yellow
hard hat to the store next door to get sandwiches and
drinks for his fellow workers, taking his time to chat
with neighbors.

Right away on the advice of two neighbors who
work in a windshield factory, I found a job there on
the evening shift. I applied at 9 a.m. on Monday, and
at 3 p.m. I found myself wearing a blue hard-hat,
glasses, sleeves and gloves (supposed to be for protection against the heat) near a furnace among a group
of guys running, sweating, and putting glass on racks
which are conveyed through the furnace where the
windshields get their curved shape. It is so noisy that
hand signs and whistling are the only means of
communication most of the time. A guy comes and
explains to me how to choose, pick up, carry and set
up the glass on the racks. He stays with me ten
minutes and then leaves me alone to do the job.
Fortunately the worker who catches the glass on the
other side of the racks is more experienced and he
helps me, pointing out the glass to pick and the
measurement to set it up by, since each rack is
different. After a while you get used to it. It takes 30
seconds for the whole operation, and you soon begin
to recognize the racks and the glass that goes on them.
It helps not to waste a second looking around for the
right kind of glass because each thirty seconds a new
rack comes, and if you are too slow you have to set
the glass in the rack closer to the open furnace. Every
hour I switch with the worker who controls the lines
and catches the glass on the other side of the racks.

For me and for most of the furnace workers the work is physically at the limit of our possibilities. There's not only the weight of the glass but the constant work in extreme heat with only two 15 minute breaks a night. You may wonder how there are people to do such a job. In fact the turnover rate is very high and the company is constantly hiring new workers, some of them quitting the very same day. But since unemployment is very high in our area, there are always people in such need for money that they accept to do anything. It seems that the company does not interest itself with the conditions of work, preferring to give extra money for the job than to make it more bearable. And the workers find it normal since it is well paid. You can always quit if you don't like it, people say.

Once I asked the evening plant manager if they couldn't fix the fans that are supposed to blow the hot air away above the furnace. He didn't see the necessity because they find the motors able to stand the heat. Human beings are more easily replaceable. The union steward, whom I had asked at least to do something so that we wouldn't all be burned to a crisp, told me that the union couldn't do anything because the matter was not mentioned in the contract. The lack of concern for others is what is hardest to bear, and the attitude affects nearly all of us. With the production-oriented mentality most of us are just able to do strictly what we were supposed to do regardless of the consequences for the others. But then, what a smile from God in this small hell when someone gives an extra hand to you, or to anybody.

You see we have a place here even though this is called the richest country in the world. Recently an article in a Detroit newspaper pointed out that this type of boring and frustrating work is a main cause of homicide here. Detroit, in spite of its high wages, is the murder capital of the world.

Sam:

Our neighborhood is 40% white and 40% black and 20% latino, that is, Mexican and Puerto-Rican. Of the whites many are Appalachians and many Maltese. In recent years there has been a vast migration of Appalachians, blacks from the south, and Latin Americans to industrial centers like Detroit in the hope of finding work. Now the present crisis has hit Detroit particularly hard, for it's a city that depends almost entirely on one industry, automobile making. Our unemployment rate is the highest in the country.

In our fraternity here the mail to answer, visitors to receive, along with the desire to be more part of the neighborhood, led us to think that one of us ought to have more free time so that we could do these things without tension or cutting into our time of prayer. So, for the last two months, I have been working only part-time in the foundry. Besides the letters and household chores, I have time to do a few odd jobs in the neighborhood and be generally more present to the people here. I have also planted a garden behind our house which is my pride and joy. I derive an altogether inordinate pleasure from it. We invite anyone who might be near to come and taste our tomatoes and smell our roses.

Eric is working at a box factory. He began there as a fork-lift operator, then he helped to make the boxes for a while and now he's driving a truck to deliver the boxes to different places in and around the city. Brother Roger, as you know has gone to live in a little apartment in an all-black neighborhood. He's still working at the hospital as an orderly. We find it very enriching for the fraternity that we live the reality of the ghetto through Roger. Not living together brings of course a problem of communications but we manage to get together often.

Roger:

The outward appearance of my neighborhood is rather forbidding: decrepit and abandoned houses, empty lots where houses have been torn down, dirty streets, strewed with debris of all kinds. On other streets you see houses with well-kept yards where sleek Cadillacs stand beside rusty jalopies. It seems dead around the abandoned buildings, but the ghetto is full of life. Near the shops and liquor stores it can swarm with high-spirited crowds. In the summertime people play cards on the sidewalk and barbeque their spareribs in front of their houses. When two cars pass each other in the street and the people in them know each other, they stop to chat as though they were on their doorsteps, and if you are behind them it is better for you not to blow your horn. Time is not something that counts for the unemployed. The day is like the night and the night like the day. Late at night or early in the morning someone may well knock on your door to ask for some small favor.

It was easy for me to find an apartment. Drawn by a sign on the wall of a building which said, "low rent," I took an apartment on the third floor of this three story building. It was only after having paid my rent that I understood why the rent was so low: it rained in the living room. That didn't bother me too much because there were other rooms where it didn't rain. Since then, though, the roof has been repaired.

A white man living in such a neighborhood is necessarily suspect. People wondered if I had guns or was a police informer. I had more than my share of break-ins, though thieves are not racists. Tired of replacing the lock they kept breaking, I found it more economical to leave the key attached to the door frame. Since I did that, they don't come any more. Actually, they never took much because they never found much to take. Perhaps they just came out of curiosity.

After a year in the neighborhood the people have gotten used to seeing me. A few neighbors know me from having worked with me in the hospital. Many know that a room in my apartment has been turned into a chapel. A Catholic "Brother" is not a familiar notion for them; they conclude that I am a "Preacher"! There are many little churches in the neighborhood which are very poor and where the pastor, or "preacher" has a very humble job which enables him to live and support his family. The preacher in a nearby church is a mailman, another collects the garbage at the hospital where I work. The people take me for one of them too.

It is still among the blacks in this country that one finds the greatest number of poor people, and that's why I've looked for a way to come and settle in the ghetto. It must be kept in mind that not so long ago they were slaves. They do not forget it. Slavery has left wounds which can only heal slowly. The racism which resulted has also caused wounds, and even if it has lost its vigor, it has not completely disappeared, and legislation is not enough to make it disappear.

From a Little Sister of Jesus living as a
Voluntary Prisoner in a prison in Switzerland:

In this letter I would like to tell you about my

stay in prison. It is difficult to write about everything that we have lived together, for I do not want to lack discretion and respect for my companions. Nevertheless I will try to give you a true picture of what our live is like.

First of all it is important to say that my companions suffer and that in order to understand this suffering we must live it with them. Each one has her load of problems, her emotional life and family life, shattered or unbalanced.

Each one may write letters as often as she likes as long as she is able to buy the writing paper and stamps with her pocket money. But many have no one to write to or never receive an answer. This suffering and solitude in such a closed world is hard to bear. It is sometimes completely unendurable and it explains the violent reactions, which are like a cry of despair in order to safeguard the little that one still does possess of herself.

This is the portion of wretchedness that each one wakes up to every morning and has to drag along until she can finally go back to sleep again. But many sleep very little or very badly.

Yet there are also wonderful moments of sharing and helpfulness which amaze us. In prison we are all materially poor; money has no power. Sharing obliges the one who wants to share to give something she herself really needs. It has often reminded me of the widow's mite or the broken vase of perfume.

What hurts me the most is to see that prison puts our friends into situations that seem without solution. Most of them are young, and life in prison marks them with a deep sense of disgust and revolt. They often feel rejected by a society which does not know how to cope with them, and by their families and friends as well. They have the impression that they are condemned, classified and despised, and this cannot help destroying something in a human person. One can see essential moral values being destroyed in them — love, trust, self-confidence. It is painful to watch.

A little sister among them should be an unfailing sign of hope, weak of course, but always true and always there. In prison we must love even when all seems hopeless, have unlimited confidence, yet be careful not to let ourselves be taken in. We must always have great hope for our companions but realize too their limits and faults just as we know our own. With that as a starting-point we try to go forward with them, helping them to discover what is most beautiful in themselves. Yes, we must try to be a sign of love for them, to be a reflection of the merciful attentiveness of Jesus, to love them for no other reason than love.

Our day consists of nine hours of work with a break for the midday meal plus another hour of rest. After the evening meal the cells remain open for a while and we can talk to each other. It is a friendly moment. Each cell includes a bed, cold water, and a toilet. In all it measures about six by nine feet.

Work is the type that can be done in a factory, small workshops of packing or assembly work, or laundry, sewing, knitting, etc. There has to be a certain output, which is taken into account when the monthly report is made. These reports affect whether we are able to order soap, cigarettes, coffee, writing paper, stamps, and so on. They also figure when parole is considered.

The food is eatable and sufficient, but there is not much variety. Sunday lunch is better prepared.

For my companions Saturdays, Sundays and

other days off are very long because we have to stay in our cells nearly all day long except for meals. Many dread these days when they are alone with themselves.

To take our mind off things we are allowed three books every two weeks. Twice a week we can watch television, on Friday, Saturday, or Sunday evening, depending on the program, which we cannot choose either. But each can have her own transister radio — this is something new.

Before leaving prison, each one can look for a job and a room with the help of the social worker. The staff, although not always qualified for this work, does try to do the best for each one. But prison itself being a bad thing, our friends reject everything including the staff. This is very discouraging for the warders and is a cause of the high turnover of staff.

My position is much more simple, but less comfortable. After the first few days the majority of our companions realize, I think, that it is love that we, the little sisters, want to bring them. Each one has such a thirst for love and respect! In this domain there is always the possibility of sharing and communication between us. Our friendships are often beautiful and moving. I can truly say that at the end of my stay I had come into contact with each of my companions more or less deeply. For someone who is not aware that "Jesus is the Master of the impossible," you might wonder how I did it.

When we look at each one's life, it seems made up of so much bad luck. It is a mystery why they do not have the right to a bit of peace and harmony in their lives. I try to be here, as everywhere, simply "a smile on the world." How much littleness it requires.

I entrust the people of the prisons to your prayers, those here and anywhere else in the world.

The communion of saints is a reality that we can almost touch in prison, and we need to believe in it with all our hearts because in this communion the help we bring our fellow-prisoners is real.

Pentecost: Little Sister Yvette, wrote to the Little Sisters of the Gospel, when she was their prioress:

We know that we have to live through and from the living Christ. We have to live the absolute love that the Son has for his Father and for men. We know that our friendship with our brothers must well up from God's own heart, for he gives us a new heart molded in the spirit of the Beatitudes. We know that the bonds of our love for one another are a source of joy and communion and that in the Spirit they can build unity among all men — universal love.

On the day of our religious profession we received a mission. Our mission and our consecration were given to us at the same time and indissolubly linked. It is the mission to tell the Good News of Jesus, to be messengers of the Spirit of fire and love, whose role is to bring Life, the life of grace that Jesus came to spread in abundance. He sends us. He wants us for heralds of the kingdom.

Contemplation and evangelization are indissolubly linked for us.

Our whole being is consecrated to God *for* His works *however* He wants it of us.

To be sure, we are young and most of us are just starting on the path of giving ourselves totally to God and our brothers. Our fraternities for the most part are just opening.

In most places the Little Sisters are still working on the study of the language and the discovery of the way of thinking and the values in the culture, family and society of their friends.

May it be with Jesus' eyes that we look at His poor. And He is the one who will tell us then how far to go.

Don't let us limit our vocation, whatever we do. Don't limit it out of fear that we won't know what to do or how to do it, or what not to do. That's a problem we'll have to look for a solution to when it arises.

Don't limit it by narrow-mindedness. Perhaps you're reacting to things from the past in the Church that may have made you suffer, like badly placed missionary gestures for example. It would be wrong to become so we no longer dare to announce Jesus:

And I'm anxious about this most of all: don't let us close our hands and our hearts on the love the Spirit gives, with its two-way movement. It carries us back to its source, to the Father of mercies pouring out His love through Jesus. And it carries us on with His work, His movement of spreading His own presence.

To think only of intimacy and union with God, even if your sharing of the life and work of poor people is very real, would be to mistake the nature of love. You would be stopping the expansive movement that Love is made of, for it asks us to be its messengers.

On the other hand, if the weak, fragile instruments that we are, at the beginning of our path, yet instruments the Spirit has chosen and sent to announce Jesus — if we do not cultivate an intimacy with the Lord that would allow us constantly to receive the lights and impulses of His Spirit of love, what would we have then, to bring to our brothers and to live along with them?

Remember Father Voillaume's book *The Need for Contemplation?* There is a passage that has always given me a lot of light on our vocation.

Father Voillaume says that the Heart of Christ is the one "place" where the two movements of love, which seem divergent, join together:

— the movement that makes us love God till we are detached from all that is created.
— the movement that makes us love men till we are totally present to their everyday earthly tasks.

He says that the contemplation of the Heart of Christ is a root from which springs a double shoot.

The first shoot is to enter into the inexpressible act by which Jesus contemplates His Father and to dwell in the prayer of adoration and intercession that wells up from its sources. Thus the Eucharist becomes the core of our lives.

The apostolate that is ours will be marked by this contemplative root; it will bear witness to a personal experience. "What our eyes have seen and our hands have touched, that is what we pass on to you," St. John wrote in his first epistle. We must announce Jesus with the direct simplicity of those who are giving testimony to what they have seen. Cut off from the root of contemplation, such simplicity would quickly turn into the sterility of empty words. I have pointed out the danger to you.

The second shoot will find expression in the simplicity with which after the example of Jesus, we will share the life of men. This is what the spirit of Nazareth means for us. We not only share people's lives, but do it with an apostolic approach that springs from the friendship that lives in the Heart of

Jesus, who desires to save all men. Separated from its root in prayer, this shoot of friendship would only produce sterile sharing of the human condition and shirking the sense of our apostolic responsibilities. This too is a risk I have spoken of.

May the Lord send his Spirit on us. May His Fire burn in us so that we know the way to be witnesses to His love and that we carry the Gospel by His strength.

Fraternities of the Gospel in the Cameroons:

Salampoubey-Weleley is 500 miles from any city in the heart of the African jungle. For seven years there have been Little Brothers and Little Sisters of the Gospel living there. There are two people in the village: pygmies (called Bakas) and settled village-dwellers (called Bagandus). They are different in race, language, culture, and economic system. The pygmies, who are a people of hunters and gatherers, get the short end of the relationship and there are many injustices.

Our task could be put this way: to live as brothers and sisters to these two peoples, to help them to get into contact with one another, to accompany them in the inevitable changes that the development of the nation they belong to will bring, to help them not to lose their own personality in these changes, and of course to help them to encounter Jesus.

The Little Brothers describe a day in the village:

Wednesday today. The dry season is starting. Like every day we get up when the rooster crows at dawn. About 6:00 the brothers gather in the village chapel for Morning Praise and then spend an hour of adoration before Jesus in the Eucharist. Gaston the elderly catechist comes to pray too. He reminds us of the old man Simeon in the Gospel, for here in this jungle too the Lord has sent witnesses before us to announce the good news. When we came, we found several Christians already here, as if the rest of the world had forgotten about them.

After prayer the brothers don't spend long chatting over breakfast. You have to start working early, for the sun will be hot and make the work harder.

Brother Jacques takes off his shirt and plants a pineapple patch close to the house. All the fruits we need, we have to grow ourselves, for there's no market or store. And there's nothing better than example for giving others new ideas. That's why we put fruit trees all around the house (lemon, grapefruit, orange, mango, pawpaw, avocado, etc.) and planted vegetables we can eat. Lots of folks started to find that a varied food supply was a good thing and asked us for seeds to plant in their fields. About 10:30 Jacques comes back to the house to do the cooking over the wood fire out behind the house. Plantain bananas are the staple of the region; the only meat is game caught in the jungle.

Meanwhile, another brother, Daniel, goes to work in the village plantation 15 minutes' walk into the jungle. It takes a machete to clear the brush out of the manioc and banana fields and you have to do it often. When he comes back to the fraternity toward 11:00, he spends two hours of attentive listening with two young friends of the village, patiently checking some tones in the conjugation of verbs. The languages of the people here have never been studied systematically or written down. Daniel is building on the

work of the brothers who've been here longer than he
and establishing a whole grammar. He's the one who
teaches Baka to the sisters and to the European nurses
who have come to take care of the dispensary.
Jacques has learned Bangandu and Gilles is working
on it too.

Gilles, who's called Ngbo-buma now, a name he
chose because it means "God loves us," spends the
morning with a dozen young Bakas, boys and girls
10-15. They've made what was formerly one of our
fields into a cooperative and the children cultivate it
in common. They sell half of what they grow and
divide the rest among them. They divide up what they
make on the sale too, Ngbo-buma is reaching out
toward all the pygmies with the model of this little
cooperative. At present there's a schism between the
young and the grown-ups. The grown-ups are people
formed by nomadic life in the jungle. They hold onto
their ancestral communitarian values. The young
have lived almost all their lives in the village along the
road and are partially sedentarized. They are less
attracted by jungle life and yet they aren't real village-
dwellers. The communal plantation is meant to be an
initiation to agriculture, an encouragement to work,
and a chance to learn how to earn money and what to
do with it.

The noon meal together gives the brothers a
chance to share what's gone on in the morning, the
work, the discoveries among the people. Together as
we exchange and listen to one another, we can
discover the directions to take in our work and in our
activities, but also in our mode of being present and
our mode of evangelizing.

In the afternoon three young catechists get together with Jacques and Ngbo-Buma to prepare the

Sunday liturgy and the children's catechism. The meeting begins with a dialogue sharing on a Gospel passage. Bruno the catechist prepares the homily. Next they organize the catechism session for three other villages. We are just beginning to form the first generation of Christians.

Just before evening Daniel sets out for Ngondo, a village three miles away. He'll spend two days there with pygmy friends, a young couple. Tomorrow he'll lend a hand with building their house. He'll also speak to the Bakas of the whole village about the government tax, which they're going to have to pay for the first time. They don't much understand why they have to pay when they are so poor.

Jacques takes his bike and goes to visit a Bagandu nearby and chat awhile. There's a neighbor who owns goats that are doing a lot of damage in the village by getting into the fields. It's a source of feuds between Bagandus and Bakas. The neighbor had asked Jacques to help him look for a solution to his problem.

Ngbo-buma is on the porch with neighbors who come to sit and smoke and talk, until at last the conversations are interrupted by the arrival of the little sisters for mass. They are followed by some of those who became Christians long ago (Bagandus) from the nearest hamlet. The Bakas go back home; the Christians go into the chapel. By the light of the gas lamp you can see the walls with their paintings of traditional symbolic motifs. We love to pray there, prostrate before Jesus in the Eucharist, presence of God-Love among the poor of our jungle.

We are there to pray and intercede in the name of all our friends around us. A few among the Bagandus in our village are just beginning to discover the Good

News of salvation in Jesus Christ. The vast majority still have no idea who Jesus is. Only the Spirit of the living God can open hearts to the discovery of the life that they don't yet suspect the existence of.

In the pygmy hamlet nearby, the drums re-echo and the songs of the hunters rise up toward the jungle and toward Komba (God) to thank Him for the game taken in the hunt and to express their joy at being alive.

The Little Sisters tell of camping in the jungle
With their Pygmy friends:

July and the first half of August is the time to pick wild mangoes. Bakas and Bagandus both go; they try to get a supply for the whole year. It's a fruit that resembles a mango but is smaller. The pit is used too for making gravies which all are fond of. During this period both the Bagandu and the Baka villages are practically emptied out for several weeks.

When pygmies go into the jungle, they usually travel in small groups by families and so everybody is related. We went along with our closest neighbors. There was Bayolo and Mokulabaka, the elderly couple, their married children, the two families, and Assida. Assila Mbondo and Ngamo were there with her little boy.

We set out, sacks on our backs, a few supplies of food, what we'd need to make a fire and boil water and two bunches of bananas that we gave to our friends so that everybody could have some. The women were carrying enormous baskets. They had brought along everything they have, actually not much. Most important they were bringing bananas which you can't get in the jungle, a few pots, a mat to sleep on, and squawking chickens. The men had their crossbows and all they need to start a fire without matches: flintstone, metal, kindling.

We started out through the jungle paths. You have to keep looking at your feet along these narrow trails so full of obstacles — vines and roots, tree trunks, army ants. The scenery is the same, magnificent big trees with thick underbrush and occasional swamps where you walk in the mud up to the ankle or the knee.

We stopped to rest at the beginning of the afternoon in a halting spot, and found a good-sized antelope caught in one of Assila Hbondo's traps. Rejoicing for all. Assila started butchering it while everybody looked on. Meantime Sambuku, Bayolo's son's wife, went with us to get branches and leaves to make our mongulu (hut) when we would arrive at the camp and repair two others that seemed to be falling apart a little. Two hours and it was done. Yaye had found some honey and shared it among everyone, quite a treat. The women were already cooking the meat and some bananas. They had a corner for us in the big communal mongulu, where a fire was already burning. You really need one to keep warm at night because you're almost in the open air. It was already dark when we sat down gladly with the appetites the day's work had given to a meal of antelope and mashed bananas. We spent a good night though the ground was hard, and next morning before daybreak Bayolo the elder made us a simple, lovely speech about Komba who created everything, who gave us the things of the jungle, and life, and everything. He also told everyone to be hospitable to the little sisters.

First thing in the morning we went to gather mangoes with the women. They sliced them and we removed the pits. Then we moved on to the main campsite where we stayed a week. There we discovered our friends very different from how we know them in the village. They are happy to be alive, they are "kings" of the jungle, even if their joy falls short after a hard day's gathering when they've found nothing, neither meat nor roots.

Every morning after a breakfast of bananas and meat, when there is some, each one sets out hunting or gathering. We go along with the women to pick mangoes, to look for roots or to fish in the streams when there's not enough meat. They come back three or four hours later with heavy bundles of wood for the evening's cooking. The men go to check their traps, try to catch a bird or shoot a monkey with their bows, look for honey or termites.

Before sunset everybody comes back to camp. There is joy or dejection according to what each one brings with him. But everything is shared among all, provided the families are getting along well together. In the evening the women fix supper, the children go to the spring for water, the men help take the pits out of the mangoes or just rest. The talk is gay and loud with everyone joining in from wherever he is, but all can hear for the huts are close together. The two of us have our mongulu. At nightfall someone nearly always brings us a share of their supper. Then everyone goes to bed and it is our chance to have a longer time of prayer. Some evenings one or another tells a story. They enjoy that a lot. Or you can hear someone asking God for food for tomorrow, or sometimes in the middle of the night several women start singing the Yeli (the women's songs) to still a crying child or call forth game for the men's great hunt — gorillas, monkeys, bears, elephants.

It's life in the open, sometimes a harsh life, for

our friends. But we sense it is a life that simplifies you and brings you very close to the providence Jesus speaks of in the Gospel.

Yet we wonder how our friends can come little by little to know the God of Jesus Christ and the Word he speaks to us.

We are very poor and helpless among them, faltering when we speak their language, lost in the jungle after twelve yards. Picking fruits, gathering wood, digging for roots a yard or two down — we have everything to learn from them. Walking for hours in the jungle — life is hard, for them as well as for us.

We are looking for ways now to speak to them of God since some of them are waiting for it and ask us to. We thought of beginning with creation since they believe precisely in a God who is one and who gave them all the things of the jungle. But there are ambiguities since their God was a man and had several wives and children. And then abstract reflection is foreign to them; they can't make much sense out of it. But we believe that just because they are poor the God of Jesus Christ, who is Love, can come and reveal Himself to them, to the overflowing of their hearts. Pray hard, little sisters around the world, that we let Jesus encounter them, as He said in the Gospel of yesterday's mass:

> "I thank you Father, for you have hidden these things from the wise and learned and revealed them to the little."[6]

*From the Little Sisters of the Gospel
In Cawood, Kentucky:*

This has been the hardest winter in anyone's memory here in the Appalachian mountains, and we felt as if it was locking the hill-people still more into their isolation and their sense of helplessness. For several months there was a snow storm at least once a week, and Anne Marie and I often missed a day of work because we couldn't get into town. We kept busy making quilts on days like that, a skill we've learned from neighbor ladies.

One neighbor came and asked us to teach her to knit. Maybe she was just looking for a way to make the time go by, though she and her children could badly use warm sweaters. She started off well, but then she lost her yarn or misplaced her needles or had another difficulty and finally gave up. Maybe some day she'll try again.

Like everybody we needed more coal this year to try to keep warm with. It was hard to get it delivered. The Red Cross even had to set up an emergency service so that people could get a little coal. It's ironic in this region so exploited by the coal mines. Now that spring is coming we have floods to fear when the heavy snows melt, because the method of mining here is a particularly ruthless one that strips off the ground cover and the forests, leaving no protection against floods and landslides.

Our neighbors come in and out of the fraternity all day long, to use the phone or just to change scenes for a little while and get a bit of distraction. Little Joe comes sometimes for help with his homework. Now his mother wants us to teach her to read. Is she serious or is it a way to pass the time? In any case just her idea is something positive. Our friends carry a terrible weight in their lives.

Our fraternity in Cawood can well be called the "slow mission." We penetrate gradually by the friendship between our neighbors and us, in a simple dialogue of our lives. We live a mutual help and simple sharing that always boils down to the essential: our friendship with the Lord through His Word and His gifts which He offers to all.

There are two seasons here in Cawood, as in many parts of the world, the cold season and the warm. In the warm season the contacts are easy and numerous. That's when we have to open up the pathways of friendship we'll still be able to walk on in winter when everybody stays indoors and people rarely go out on foot.

It's by conversations that it would be easy to call "village gossip" that we slowly learn to know the monotonous framework of simple people's lives, and also their deep drama. Shaky marriages, teenagers' problems, the materialistic and short-termed vision of life people have — we discover our mission in all of these.

It is our grace and our strength that our vocation as followers of Brother Charles allows us this slow penetration, attentive to all that goes into people's lives. But how clearly we feel that such a vocation has to be borne up and carried by our prayer and intercession so that we'll be ready not to let slip any occasion to manifest the concrete love the Lord has for his people.

Rita

Christmas. Little Sister Magdeleine writes to the Little Sisters of Jesus about spiritual childhood:

Let the mystery of Bethlehem be your light. The world has plenty of human values. The world has plenty of experts, plenty of scholars. What is missing from the world are the utterly simple qualities of gentleness and joy, trust and peace.

In His great love, Christ, the Son of God, chose to pass through a little infant's helplessness, the only state in which someone is totally given over into the hands of another. This manger of Bethlehem contains the whole Christ, God and man together, and in its extension there is the workshop of Nazareth, the passion and cross, and all the glory of the resurrection and heaven itself. The utter lowliness of the manger bears witness to Jesus' mission as savior which His death on the cross will confirm.

The world has plenty of human values already. In an age when pride, jealousy, and the will to power and wealth run wild, breeding massacres and wars, in an age when the whole world is filled with a mood of sadness, hatred, vindictiveness and mutual contempt, the message of the manger of Bethlehem will bring the world the gentleness and peace and joy that it doesn't have. To the anger and hatred in the world must come to answer, the gentleness and the smile of the infant Jesus of Bethlehem; to the arrogance in the world, the littleness and defenselessness of the newborn baby of the crib.

The mission that belongs to the Little Sisters of Jesus is to live the mystery of this crib and to carry its message of peace and gentleness, of hope and joy, from one end of the world to the other, without restricting it just to the Christmas season. They are to carry it to those who have never heard it as well as to those who have rejected it or forgotten it, and to carry it not in an official way, but just very simply as poor people would.

Be a smile on the world, on the world of the least-considered, the poorest, the most outcast. Be able to live in the midst of your fellow creatures and keep a child's heart, a child's soul, with eyes that see every-

thing simply and frankly, even evil. Cross tightly
closed borders without danger of making anyone
nervous, no more than a little child bothers grown-
ups, who need not fear his influence or his rational
arguments or his harsh judgments, since he is so little
that he can't think himself somebody to be noticed.

The first Christmas message was the announce-
ment of the angel to shepherds: "I bring you tidings of
great joy. Today is born to you a Savior who is Christ
the Lord. And you will know him by this sign: you
will find an infant in swaddling clothes lying in a
manger . . ."[7] How could we find a better means than
the one God Himself chose to make known to the
world the coming of the Savior?

The Little Brothers of Jesus write news from
Afula, a little Israeli village:

Brother Yohanan returned to our hill-top town
last winter. As many men were still engaged in the
army, he wanted first to be of use by helping out as a
postman for three months. Then there was a truce and
the majority of those mobilized were able to return
home and take up their habitual occupations again.
So Yohanan returned to his pottery workshop, and
his friends in the neighboring small workshops were
glad to see him.

Brother Paul is already touching on his sixth
year of work with the cheese factory. It's situated in
the fertile valley of Yezreel, on the site where Gideon
once stood up to the Midianites with his 300 men,
with jars and torches and trumpets. Paul works at the
factory as a locksmith and general handyman.

As for me, I'm equally faithful to my stocking
factory, although just now the factory is going

through a bad time. For a small town like Afula, the closing down of a factory is not without consequences. It's not just a "problem" but a matter of human beings, men and women who are my work-mates, and who are worried about the future.

We've made a little hermitage so that each of us can go away and pray from time to time. It's on the Mount of Beatitudes, north of Lake Tiberias. Myself. I try to go there two sabbaths each month. It's one of those places that remind you in a simple and evocative way of the concrete details of Jesus' healing ministry and of the core of His message. You brothers who know me well will remember that I asked to come here to the Holy Land specially to pray for Israel and the world, hoping to end my days here. It's good to labor humbly in the deafening noise of a large factory, sharing the life of the people around us. And it's good to retire into the silence of the hills, especially when the hill in question may well be the one where Jesus used to retire and spend the night in prayer.

In the present circumstances at an important and critical time, you feel more than ever urged to retire into the silence of prayer and intercession.

Since the October war there's a mixture of anxiety, confusion, weariness, and hope — a feeble and timid hope for that genuine peace which everyone so ardently desires, though of course not everyone has the same ideas on the concrete form this peace should take. But at least it's the first time since Israel came into existence that peace is no longer an empty dream, even if the road is bound to be a long one still. And there remain the obstacles of egoism, prejudice, and tragic mutual misunderstanding, which no doubt will need still more tears and suffering to overcome.

The problem of the Palestinians, among others, remains totally unsolved. It's a deeply tragic situation. For violence brings more violence in its wake, terrorist raids lead to counter-raids, and the bitter cycle continues. The worst perhaps is that hearts become hardened and hate is sown on both sides. In my little world of the factory, thank God, Jews and Arabs still work together. Up till now relations are good, and the atmosphere is, or seems at least, friendly. But this is not the case everywhere in town.

Among people who are simple and possess little, fear and panic easily arise, more so than in the kibbutzim and the bigger towns. Here at Afula we've had several alerts, some real, some false, and that leaves its mark on the population. A minimum of precautionary measures had to be taken, so civilian guards were requisitioned for day and night duty. Yohanan, being an Israeli citizen, was called like everyone else. Don't worry, he goes his rounds quite unarmed. But still, it's not a cheerful affair.

As for us, we try to bear all this in silence, prayer and supplication, in charity and hope. And it's not always easy to do. We are weak men, and our spontaneous reactions are not always those of Jesus nor those He would wish us to have. But we do our best, and try to review our life together over and over in the light of the Gospel. We suffer, and we share the sufferings of those who suffer and weep, whether on this side or that.

A Little Sister of Jesus writes
From the Fraternity in Glasgow:

When we moved into the flat on a small housing scheme, we had been given much advice and many warnings about the difficulties of living and working in a place where there might be a lot of mixed feelings and barriers of prejudice due to the fact that we were nuns, wearing a religious dress. As for going to work in a factory, that seemed hard to believe.

We hadn't been there for many days, before it became a vital necessity to find work if we were to pay our first rent bill and other bills that come when one moves, so we looked in the newspapers and spent a few days job-hunting. When I inquired in the factories of our nearby industrial estate, two of the young girls from our parish came with me. Aware of the situation in Glasgow, we weren't very hopeful of finding a job, and they naturally took me to the Catholic firms first. We tried several but without any luck. Our last hope was a shirt factory, but the girls didn't think it was possible, as the owner wasn't a Catholic. The young man who interviewed me passed no comment on the fact that I was a nun. He treated me like anyone else applying for a job, and told me to apply again on May 1st. Of course between then and May 1st I tried other places, but unsuccessfully. However, to be interviewed on St. Joseph's feast day was reassuring, and you can imagine our delight when I got the job.

I worked there for nine months and although I've worked in several factories before as a little sister, I've never loved it as much as I loved it there. At first they didn't know what to expect with a nun working in their midst, but it didn't take long to find out that I was very ordinary — I had to be shown all the ropes and learn the work. We had many a good laugh and often enjoyed singing. Then there were so many signs of affection, which made me feel I was one of them — from members of both Churches. Indeed it was months before I even knew the different denominations of my co-workers because one was as warm-hearted as another. When the first holidays came, I wasn't entitled to holiday pay, but imagine my surprise at getting an envelope from all the girls with money for the holidays. They had made a collection.

What I am saying about the girls in this factory doesn't seem extraordinary to them. I knew I wasn't getting special treatment, because I was so often struck by their kindness and friendliness towards one another, and religion certainly wasn't a barrier to their friendship. Before leaving, I even made a black clerical shirt for our Bishop, and the girls helped me with it — on the understanding that the Bishop would say a prayer for them!

Leaving was a wrench, and not without tears. Their friendship was proved to me on my return to Glasgow six months later. I didn't go back to my job, as I was to stay at home at the fraternity and look after the house, but I went and invited them to a Mass on August 15. The Bishop was to celebrate it and I would renew my vows.

About twenty girls from the factory came. The ceremony was on a Friday evening, and none of them lived nearby. What is more, there was a bus strike. Some came in taxis; others, after waiting and waiting for the bus, finally hitch-hiked to the church, and afterwards told the Bishop, "We decided to travel the way Sister does." Most of them weren't Catholics.

You might say this is unusual after what one hears about the prejudice in Scotland. But we've found the same capacity for friendship among so many people on the housing scheme. Many of our friends belong to the Church of Scotland and we've come to know the ministers and their families. Last Easter after the service in their church they sent the

flowers from the altar for our little chapel in the
fraternity.

I remember when L. S. Magdeleine wrote to us,
"I have so often repeated that if I were told to define
the mission of the Fraternity in one single word, I
would not hesitate to cry: 'Unity' because unity sums
up everything . . . Love cannot exist without unity. To
love means seeking to be one with those we love . . .
Unity is the highest summit of love and this is why the
Beloved Lord after the Last Supper chose to end by
this prayer, 'Father, may they all be one, as you are in
me and I am in you, may they be completely one!'"

Father Voillaume:

Little Brother Charles of Jesus would see his
place in the life of the Church as a very humble one. It
is so like the life of Jesus.

What the Fraternity, and that means each one of
us, ought to show to the world is really a way of
being: social humility, sharing the common lot of men
without any privileges, being obliged to work to earn
our living, being near to the poor, alternating times of
retreat with times back in the thick of the crowds. All
these values can be lived authentically in a religious
state of life.

This is a very humble role in the evangelization
of the world. It does however announce Christ by a
certain way of being, and is an important part in the
mission of the Church. Our way of life is a message in
itself. But we will not be able to realize this exterior
way of life unless our interior attitudes correspond to
our exterior witness. We must become truly gentle,
merciful, simple, and full of respect for all men.

The Fraternity has been founded at a time in history when most men are thinking that the Church is too much of a temporal power. Its witness comes at the right time. By this I mean that the way of evangelization of the Fraternity, our way of announcing the Lord is by "poor means": respect for the poor, friendship, discretion, purely spiritual means. By not counting on efficacy and human strength, we bear witness that it is God who is at work. This way of living underlines that the Church, which we represent officially, is a spiritual power which must announce the Gospel to mankind without refusing the law of abasement which is that of the Cross of Jesus.

Part I

Chapter Three

1. Letter to a friend.

Chapter Four

1. Summer of 1902.

Chapter Five

1. See John 12:24.
2. Matthew 25:40.
3. Luke 22:19.

Part II

1. Retreat of 1905.

Chapter One

1. Henry de Castries was an officer of the French army who devoted his life to historical and geographical studies on Morocco. Brother Charles had met him at the time in his life when he too was a Moroccan explorer. When Brother Charles returned to the Sahara many years later, he got back into touch with de Castries and later became for him a spiritual counsellor.
2. See Mark 12:28-34.
3. Letter to a Trappist monk, June 8, 1892.

Chapter Two

1. November 8, 1897.
2. December 25, 1894.

2. The purpose of this general chapter was to reunite the several branches of the Cistercian Order, of which the Trappists were one. This reunification necessarily required modifications in the rules of the abbeys of each branch. Brother Charles feared that it might lead to a mitigation, which in his eyes would be a decadence. In fact, the reform remained quite austere, and Brother Charles acknowledged this.

4. September 12, 1892.

5. Retreat at Ephrem, April 26, 1900.

6. Henry Duveyrier was a Saharan explorer who had helped Brother Charles get ready for his Moroccan exploration at a time when nobody else put much confidence in him. Brother Charles kept for Duveyrier a deeply grateful friendship.

7. John 1:39.

8. John 21:23.

9. Meditations on the Gospel, written while Brother Charles was at Nazareth, 1897-1899.

Chapter Three

1. June 6, 1896, to Mme. de Bondy.

2. Nowadays the Trappists too have only one category of monks and have done away with the category of "lay brothers."

3. See Luke 7:47.

4. November 8, 1896.

Chapter Four

1. August 2, 1896.

2. Luke 12:49.

3. John 12:26.

4. Mark 6:3.

5. Matthew 11:29.
6. Luke 2:51.
7. Philippians 2:8.
8. Matthew 18:3.
9. Romans 12:21.
10. Romans 2:11.
11. Diary, July 22, 1905.
12. The only person who tried to follow him, Brother Michel, got sick and had to leave after only a few weeks. Yet Brother Michel had the stamina to join a Carthusian monastery afterwards, where he lived into his eighties. Father Huvelin had judged rightly: Brother Charles's rule was far too austere.
13. John 12:26.
14. John 13:15.
15. Luke 6:40.
16. 1909.

Chapter Five

1. January 27, 1897.
2. Luke 2:51.
3. John 1:46.
4. Acts 5:29.
5. Retreat at Nazareth, 1897.
6. Meditation on the Gospel.
7. John 13:16, Matthew 10:24, Luke 6:40, John 15:20.
8. John 14:6.
9. John 12:47.
10. Meditation on Mark 6:1-6.
11. To Mme. de Bondy, November 4, 1891.
12. To a Trappist monk, November 16, 1891.
13. To the same monk, June 8, 1892.

14. July 3, 1891.
15. Mark 6:3.
16. Directory, 1909.
17. Constitutions, 1896.
18. Constitutions, 1901.
19. June 6, 1903.
20. Constitutions, 1896.
21. John 13:34-35.
22. Rule of the Little Brothers, 1902.
23. Matthew 11:29.
24. Luke 2:51.
25. Philippians 2:8.
26. Constitutions, 1901.
27. Luke 10:16.
28. Retreat at Ephrem, 1898.
29. Retreat at Ephrem, 1898.
30. Diary, 1905.
31. Rule of the Little Brothers.

Chapter Six

1. Constitutions of the Little Brothers of the Sacred Heart, 1901.
2. Meditation, March 15, 1897.
3. December 2, 1901.
4. December 30, 1901.
5. September 16, 1891, to Father Huvelin.
6. "You were no closer," he says, but of course the mode of presence is different. Brother Charles speaks here and in many of his other meditations using the language of Love, touching and often imprecise, not meant to be theologically rigorous. The presence of Jesus in the Eucharist is a real presence, but of another kind than His presence in time and space when He lived on earth.

7. Retreat at Nazareth, 1897.
8. Letter to a priest in France, May 3, 1906.

Chapter Seven

1. September 20, 1889.
2. November 4, 1889.
3. Retreat at Nazareth, 1897.
4. February 1, 1898.
5. Letter to a Trappist monk, February 15, 1898.
6. Meditation on Holy Week, written at Nazareth.
7. Meditation on the Psalms, 1897. These are the words of a man who was not always in easy transports and wrote a few months later, "Dryness and darkness, everything is hard for me: holy communion, praying, everything, everything, even to tell Jesus I love Him." (June 6, 1897) Brother Charles was just someone determined to be wholly penetrated by the light of faith.
8. Colossians 1:24.
9. Luke 6:13.
10. Galatians 2:20.

Chapter Eight

1. To his cousin, May 26, 1890.
2. To Father Huvelin, January 17, 1891.
3. June 5, 1893.
4. February 4, 1892.
5. To Mme. de Bondy, March 19, 1896.
6. To Mme. de Bondy, June 24, 1896.
7. January 24, 1897.
8. Luke 10:16.
9. Meditation on the Gospel, written at Nazareth.
10. Written at Rome, 1896.
11. John 4:34.

12. September 9, 1898.
13. In a letter to Father Huvelin, March 3, 1898.
14. To Father Huvelin, October 15, 1898.
15. To Father Huvelin, October 22, 1898.
16. To Father Jerome, January 2, 1899.
17. August 26, 1903.

Chapter Nine

1. Retreat before his ordination to the priesthood, 1901.
2. April 8, 1905.
3. Matthew 18:12-13, etc.
4. Matthew 9:12, etc.
5. Rule, 1901.
6. March 30, 1903.
7. Matthew 23:9.
8. Genesis 1:26.
9. Matthew 25:40.
10. 1 Corinthians 9:22.
11. Luke 12:49.
12. To Henry de Castries, June 23, 1901.
13. Luke 22:27.
14. Retreat at Beni-Abbès, 1902.
15. To Bishop Guérin, September 30, 1902.
16. Meditation on Matthew 9:18-19, written at Nazareth.
17. Diary, 1909.
18. To Mme. de Bondy, January 7, 1902.
19. To Mme. de Bondy, August 29, 1902.
20. To Bishop Guérin, January 19, 1902.

Chapter Ten

1. To Father Huvelin, December 13, 1903.
2. May 15, 1904.

3. To Bishop Guérin, July 2, 1907.
4. To Mme. de Bondy, December 1907.
5. February 2, 1903.
6. March 6, 1903.
7. Matthew 25:40.
8. Letter to a friend, August 1, 1916.

Chapter Eleven

1. Rule, 1901.
2. Daily Notes, 1916.
3. Retreat of 1902.
4. Retreat of 1904.
5. To Father Huvelin, December 15, 1902.
6. Rule of 1901.
7. Meditation on Luke 1:39, written at Nazareth.
8. April 8, 1905, letter to a priest in France.
9. Meditations on Mark 5:18-19.
10. Diary, 1905.
11. Retreat, 1902.
12. Quoted in the biography of Brother Charles by René Bazin.
13. Quoted in the biography of Brother Charles by Gilbert Ganne.
14. Letter to a priest, 1912.
15. To Rene Bazin, 1916.
16. May 13, 1911.
17. To Mme. de Bondy, July 20, 1914.
18. To a priest in France, June 9, 1908.
19. Matthew 28:19.
20. Directory, 1909.
21. Meditations of the Gospel.

Chapter Twelve

1. John 12:24.

2. December 15, 1904.
3. July 31, 1909.
4. October 13, 1909.
5. October 31, 1909.
6. To Mme. de Bondy.

Part III

1. Matthew 13:33.
2. Galatians 2:20.
3. John 6:29.
4. Mark 4:26.
5. Exodus 3:7-8.
6. Matthew 11:25.
7. Luke 2:10-12.